MW00776295

Real Natures and
Familiar Objects

Real Natures and Familiar Objects

Crawford L. Elder

A Bradford Book
The MIT Press
Cambridge, Massachusetts
London, England

This book was set in Palatino by SNP Best-set Typesetter Ltd., Hong Kong, and was printed and bound in the United States of America.

Library of Congress Cataloging-in-Publication Data

Elder, Crawford.
  Real natures and familiar objects / Crawford L. Elder.
    p.   cm.
  "A Bradford book."
  Includes bibliographical references and index.
  ISBN 0-262-05075-7 (hc: alk. paper)
  1. Knowledge, Theory of. 2. Ontology. I. Title.
BD161.E43   2004
110—dc22

                                    2003059684

10 9 8 7 6 5 4 3 2 1

To Carol, Brad, and Jared

Contents

III **Toward a Robust Common-sense Ontology**   129

Introduction

This book defends, with qualifications, the ontology of common sense. It argues that we exist, in ontological strictness—no paraphrase of the statement "human beings exist" is needed to show it true of the world as it really is—and that we are, in ontological strictness, surrounded by many of the medium-sized objects which common sense believes in, including some artifacts. Moreover this book argues that our cognitive relation to our surroundings is much as common sense supposes it to be. We often manage, that is, to learn a great deal about familiar objects of this or that kind just because our observations of individual members of that kind catch sight of properties which members of that kind have by nature—properties which any member is bound to possess, so long as it exists at all. Familiar medium-sized objects not only exist, then, but have essential properties, in the traditional sense, and we often are able to determine which properties are essential to one or another of nature's kinds. It is the latter claims that the book defends first, in part I.

In the seventy-eight years since Moore's "Defence of Common Sense" (Moore 1925), familiar medium-sized objects have largely disappeared from ontology, at least among analytic philosophers. They have been crowded out by sleeker rivals unheard of by common sense—objects having crisper extinction conditions, or characterized by properties not susceptible to sorites arguments, or objects whose causal efficacy traces to far cleaner laws than would ever fit common-sense objects. The approach of this book will be to argue that these replacement objects have only the weakest credentials as posits of an empirical understanding of how the world works—or have impeccable credentials, but only as posits of a badly incomplete understanding. Thus the book will take for granted a general conviction that ontology should operate under empirical load—that it should give special weight to the objects and properties we in fact treat as real in our best predictions and explanations of what happens in the world, be it at the level of everyday thought or of learned scientific theory.

This starting point is just mildly controversial. It entails for example that there is a strong presumption *against* the doctrine known as "unrestricted mereological composition" or "mereological universalism." This is the doctrine that the mereological sum of any real objects, however seemingly unrelated they may be, is an object in its own right. Thus, on the assumption that the microparticles of physics are genuine objects, the doctrine holds that there is an object composed of seventeen microparticles in my left elbow, forty-three microparticles at the bottom of the Marianas Trench, one microparticle in the star Sirius, and the entirety of the Navy's latest Ohio-class submarine. Neither folk theories nor learned theories about how the world works find any need or use for such randomly assembled "objects"—to put it mildly. So it follows, from my starting conviction, that a heavy burden of proof lies on those who wish to argue *in favor of* mereological universalism. This is mildly controversial, since in many contemporary discussions it is assumed that the burden of proof lies on those who *oppose* that doctrine.

For all that, I think that my starting presumption will seem *only* mildly controversial, at least in the general formulation I have so far given it. For the ontologists who recognize only the crisply defined objects unheard of to common sense often see themselves as engaging in something much like scientific theory building. The real controversy comes when one lists the specific topics on which, as ontologists, we must attend to the tellings of experience, and separates them from the topics on which we are free to settle answers by stipulation. Is it, one might ask, open to the ontologist to stipulate extinction and persistence conditions for the objects his ontology affirms—to settle by definition that such-and-such entities can survive these changes but not those, or can be spatially deployed in certain ways but not in others, and so on? The position this book will take is that we must learn from nature where there are real necessities, real continuings, and real unities. These matters are not ours to fashion; they are fixed independently of us. This is of course a frankly realist position, and controversially so. No book should simply presume such a position, and this book will not. Part I is an extended argument for this particular sharpening of the general stance, in itself fairly uncontroversial, that ontology must operate under empirical load.

The role of part I, then, is to defend realism about essentialness in general—the idea, that is, that it is the case mind-independently that nature's objects possess specific ones of their properties essentially. But are the *familiar* objects which *common sense* believes in among nature's objects? Doubts whether such objects really exist in the world have lately been motivated by worries about causal exclusion and sorites paradoxes. Part II defends familiar objects against causal exclusion arguments, and offers a partial response to one species of sorites paradox.

Part III then takes up the task of defending positive claims as to just which of the familiar posits of common sense really exist. Chapter 7 argues that many of the artifacts in which common sense believes really do exist, as do many biological devices shaped by natural selection. Chapter 8 defends the position that we exist, and are ourselves endowed with many abilities shaped by natural selection—and thus that our existence involves the existence as well of genes and populations and language communities.

I am grateful to Nick Zangwill, Margaret Gilbert, and Austen Clark for encouraging me to write this book. For discussions about the contents of the book, I am grateful to Nick Zangwill (again), Nenad Miščević, Gene Mills, Mike Rea, and Tom Bontly.

But my greatest debt, as will quickly become apparent, is to my colleague Ruth Millikan. Twenty years ago I puzzled my way through a deeply unorthodox and deeply illuminating manuscript titled *Language, Thought, and Other Biological Categories*, then in press at MIT Press/Bradford Books. I returned to the book a few years later to think more closely about the last chapters, which deal with ontology. I have been thinking about them ever since, and the present book is the result. I must add that the actual, historical Ruth Millikan does not agree with all that is in this book: she questions whether modal discourse reports objective states of affairs, and positively disagrees with the conclusions of chapters 4 and 5. I console myself with the reflection that she *should* agree with the positions of this book, and that she once *appeared* to do so!

I

The Epistemology and Ontology of Essential Natures

1   Conventionalism: Epistemology Made Easy, Ontology Made Paradoxical

We manage, it seems, to learn much about the kinds and stuffs and phenomena which surround us in nature. Through attentive inspection of individual members of a given kind (or individual samples of a given stuff, or individual instances of a given phenomenon), we manage to identify properties which all members of the kind are bound to possess, so long as they exist at all. Among these are often properties, or combinations of properties, which members of no other kind can possess. But exactly *how* do we manage to identify essential natures, distinctive of nature's various kinds, stuffs, and phenomena? From what premises do we infer such conclusions? The only developed answer to this question currently on offer leads to unsettling conclusions about the ontological status of essential properties. Or to speak more precisely, it leads to unsettling conclusions not about the properties themselves that we determine to be essential to nature's kinds, but about the ontological status of their *being* essential, of their essentialness. In this chapter I will argue that these conclusions are not just unsettling but unbelievable. In the next chapter I will offer an alternative answer to the epistemological question.

Just what evidence apprises us that chromium necessarily has an atomic number of 24, that quartz crystals by nature have their molecules arranged in a certain sort of lattice, that lightning is essentially an electrical phenomenon? Not just that inspected samples uniformly present the property in question. For we manage to draw distinctions between properties which samples of a stuff or members of a kind uniformly possess, and properties which they possess by their very nature. We determine that all samples of chromium come originally from Zimbabwe or South Africa or Siberia,[1] but do not judge that coming-from-Zimbabwe (-or-South-Africa-or-Siberia) belongs to chromium's very nature—that the samples *had* to come from Zimbabwe or South Africa or Siberia. We may learn that diamonds are all marketed by a monopoly enterprise, but do not infer that they are by nature marketed in this way; we distinguish between their *being marketed by a monopoly* and their *being composed of carbon*. To put it differently, we somehow learn that counterfactuals beginning "If chromium had been present in the United States, . . ." may have completions that make them true and important from the standpoint of geology or economics or politics, whereas counterfactuals beginning "If chromium had had atomic number 79, . . ." are empty and uninformative—true only vacuously. But how?

Kripke (1972) famously argued that we learn from experience that gold essentially has atomic number 79, water necessarily has molecular structure H_2O, and that (degree of) heat is by nature (degree of) mean kinetic energy. These properties are, as science informs us, explanatorily rich— they explain other properties that gold and water have with equal uniformity, or enable us to predict uniform connections between (degree of) heat and pressure. This encourages the thought that explanatory richness is the extra premise. If samples of kind K uniformly bear property p, and p is in this way explanatorily rich, perhaps it follows that p is an essential property of kind K. But is it not also an essential property of gold that gold has a melting point of 1073°C, or that gold resists corrosion by all acids and acidic compounds except aqua regia? Perhaps explanatory richness is not a necessary condition for a property's being essential. For that matter, it does explain a good deal about diamonds that diamonds are marketed by a monopoly enterprise. It explains why they are expensive, and perhaps thereby explains why they are given as tokens of important occasions or deep feelings, and so forth. "Explanatory richness" of at least some sorts may not be sufficient—even when added to uniform occurrence—to ensure essentialness.

1.1   Do We Know "Template" Truths about Essential Natures?

So what *is* the extra premise that, when added to the uniform occurrence of p among inspected members of K, permits us to infer that p is an essential property of Ks? The only answer to this question that is now widely defended is that we combine the uniformity we empirically discover among members of K with something we somehow know about the *kind* of kind to which K belongs (McGinn 1981, pp. 157–158; Sidelle 1989; cf. Jackson 1998 on our knowledge of C-extensions). Thus it is said that we know, concerning chemical compounds such as water, that whatever the molecular structure that samples of that kind prove uniformly to possess, it is a molecular structure that samples of that kind *essentially* or *necessarily* possess.[2] It is said that we know, concerning physical elements, that if samples of physical element K prove uniformly to have atomic number x,

physical element K has atomic number x by nature. Thus do
we know that the only nonempty counterfactuals concerning K must depict K as having—or at least must be consis-
tent with K's having—just that atomic number. It might be
said we know, concerning the substances which the mineralogist studies, that whatever the molecular arrangement
that the mineralogist determines samples of such a substance uniformly to have, it is an arrangement that instances
of that substance are bound to have—as quartz is bound to
have a particular lattice arrangement.

But how do we manage to know these "template" truths
concerning the kinds of nature's kinds? Do we learn them
from experience? The thought here would have to be that
we perform a metainduction. We first infer from induction
over samples of gold that gold has atomic number 79 essentially; from induction over samples of chromium that
chromium has atomic number 24 essentially; and at length
do a metainduction over physical elements in general—
inferring that each of them is characterized essentially by
a particular atomic number. But this thought obviously
cannot be defended, at least not in just this form. For we
cannot on the present way of thinking even arrive at the
premise that gold is characterized essentially by atomic
number 79 unless we already know that conclusion to which
the metainduction is to lead—that physical elements select
an atomic number not just uniformly but by nature.

Then how might we be said to know of these template
truths? One answer might be that we exercise a direct
intellectual insight, not mediated by experience, into the
natures of the higher-order kinds—for example, "physical
elements," "chemical compounds," "mineral substances"—
into which nature's specific kinds fall. But that answer
seems fanciful, of course.

Or might we learn of such template truths by armchair reflection on our own classificatory practices? Perhaps it is just a convention of ours to individuate physical elements by atomic number, chemical compounds by molecular composition, and mineral substances by (chemical composition and) molecular arrangement (Sidelle 1989). Perhaps, that is, it is our convention *not* to judge or say that the same chemical kind is present in two envisioned scenarios—two actual contexts, or two counterfactual contexts, or a mix—unless the kind envisioned in both is envisioned as having a single molecular composition. If we do have conventions of individuation such as this, it seems plausible that upon armchair reflection we would sense *that* we have them. We would find ourselves being drawn to deny that a look-alike of water, envisioned from the armchair as existing in some scenario, were *the same* chemical stuff as water as soon as we realized we were envisioning this look-alike as having a molecular composition other than H_2O—for example, the molecular composition abbreviated as "XYZ."

1.2   Conventionalism, and Essentialness as Mind-bestowed

But if this is how we arrive at our judgments that certain properties characterize nature's kinds not just uniformly but essentially, conclusions follow that are at least disturbing. Are these judgments truly warranted? The extra information we are now pictured as adding, to the empirical finding that (say) gold uniformly displays atomic number 79, is that we will not *call* a physical element "gold again," in speaking of an envisioned counterfactual scenario, unless we manage to envision that element as having the same atomic number as we have empirically identified in actual

samples of gold. Is this enough to warrant the conclusion
that a physical element cannot or could not *be* gold, unless
it had just that atomic number? Does the fact that we would
not *call* something "gold" warrant the conclusion that that
something could not *be* gold? Well, perhaps the conventions
governing what we will *call* "gold"—our conventions for
individuating, our practices of classification—are the way
they are for a reason. Perhaps they have somehow been
shaped by the way the world is. But to call something a
"convention" is to suggest that we had latitude in adopting
it—that we could have proceeded differently. Now it is
true that that suggestion is avoided if we speak instead of
our *practices* of classification. But still there is nothing in the
view we are examining that suggests that our practices are
shaped by empirical contact with the world—and hence
nothing, barring the answer scotched above as fanciful, that
suggests that they are shaped by the way the world is.

So if our judgments of essentialness are truly to be warranted, on the view we are examining, our conventions for
calling something "the same kind again" must be seen, not
as *evidence for* its being the same kind again, but as *constitutive of* its being the same kind again (Sidelle 1989, pp. 49,
65, 67). That members of a given kind must cling to certain
properties through thick and thin, in all actual phases of
their careers and in all counterfactual scenarios, must not be
something *indicated* or *suggested* by our conventions' being
such as they are, but something that obtains *in virtue of* our
conventions' being such as they are. The essentialness of
essential properties is essentialness relative to us, relative to
our conventions or practices. The essential status of essential properties is mind-dependent.

What is disturbing about this result is the way it intersects
with the thought that the essential properties of members of

a given kind are properties which those members must retain, so long as they exist at all. If the lattice arrangement essential to quartz crystals is removed, then where a moment ago there was a quartz crystal, there will be a quartz crystal no longer—the quartz crystal will have been destroyed. If the property of containing-79-protons-in-the-nucleus disappears, where a moment ago there was a gold atom, that gold atom will have ceased to exist. But in virtue of what are these occurrences *destructions*—ceasings-to-exist—instead of mere *alterations* in something that continues? This is the same question as: in virtue of what are these *essential* properties of quartz crystals and gold atoms, and not just properties that quartz crystals and gold atoms have so far proven to have? And the answer on the present view will be: in virtue of our conventions' being such as they are (Sidelle 1998, pp. 440–441). Independently of us, there will be in the world only a play of properties, one property giving place to another and that property to another in turn. That some switches of properties amount to ceasings-to-exist, that others amount to comings-into-existence, whereas yet others amount to mere alterations, is the case only relative to us and our conventions. In other words, that the existences of the world's objects begin where they do, and end where they do, will not be independent of us and our conventions. Beginnings and endings of existence, for the world's objects, will obtain only relative to us.

Should this result be articulated in antirealist fashion, as the claim that we by our conventions actually *construct* the existences of the world's objects? Proponents of the conventionalist account of essentialness in fact divide on this question. Alan Sidelle, a prime exponent of conventionalism, provides an austere interpretation that avoids antirealism; many other exponents elect strongly antirealist formulations. My position is that either style of articulation is disturbing in its own way—indeed, if the arguments of the next section are right, conventionalism on either articulation is simply not believable.

On Sidelle's version of conventionalism, all that there is in the world, independently of us, is "stuff" (or, as a commentary on Sidelle calls it, "world-stuff").[3] World-stuff is by no means undifferentiated: it bears all manner of different properties, and throughout it particular properties routinely get replaced by other properties. But there are no objects in the world as it is independently of us. For objects are (or would be) entities that get destroyed when certain properties are replaced, and merely alter when certain other properties get replaced—objects have certain properties essentially, and others merely contingently (Sidelle 1998, p. 441; 1989, p. 55n.). And there are, in the world as it exists independently of us, no modally qualified states of affairs. Apart from world-stuff—apart from the world as it exists independently of us—there is only us. That is, there are our conventions of individuation, and (presumably) the utterances and thoughts that implement these conventions. Our making these utterances and having these thoughts create in us the impression that there are in the world objects, having certain properties essentially, but this impression is strictly false. It must be added that Sidelle's writings are tight-lipped about just what *our* existence involves—it may, for all the texts show, amount to no more than the occurrence of a series of such utterances and thoughts.

Most philosophers of generally conventionalist sympathies elect a richer picture of the world. There do exist in the world objects, on the richer sort of picture, and the existences of the world's objects have beginnings and endings. But they have these only relative to our conventions for individuation, our practices of classification. So it is in a sense true that we (by our conventions) construct, shape, the existences of the world's objects. This is of course "construction" in a transposed sense. It does not require the use of hammers and saws, and we do not do it in the sweat of our brows. We do it merely by thinking and talking as we do. And if this sounds mysterious—how, by just thinking, can we make objects arise and last for determinate periods and then cease to exist?—the answer is that the objects to which we do this are as insubstantial as our own constructing activities. They have only the shadow reality of a mental (or a linguistic) projection. But *being* just that—having no existence save existence-relative-to-our-thought-and-talk— they really are entities whose existences we delimit just by thinking and talking. There are in the world no "ready-made objects" (Putnam 1982; cf. Putnam 1981, pp. 53–54). Rather the world of objects is "a kind of play," a series of stories, of which we are the authors; we do ourselves appear in the stories, but nevertheless "the authors *in* the stories are the *real* authors" (Putnam 1977, p. 496).

1.3   How Conventionalism about Essentialness Yields Paradoxes

Are these two alternative conventionalist pictures of the world not just unsettling—or exciting, depending on one's point of view—but outright untenable? That is what I now will argue. I will begin with a paradox that confronts at least many, probably most, conventionalists who elect the antirealist picture. I will then present two parallel paradoxes, one of which confronts the rest of the conventionalists who elect the antirealist picture, the other of which confronts conventionalists who elect the austere realist picture of Sidelle.

Most philosophers nowadays subscribe to a materialist view of our minds: human mental events are by nature events befalling human brains. It is fair to infer that many, and probably most, conventionalists are committed to this general view. There are of course importantly different versions of materialism. Some hold that our mental events are brain events neurochemically specified, others that they are brain events functionally specified, yet others that they are brain events teleofunctionally specified (Millikan 1984; Elder 2001b). But all materialists—including all conventionalists who are materialists—are committed to the position that the existence in the world of human brains is logically prior to the occurrence in the world of human mental events. Human mental events are by nature events that happen in or to human brains; unless and until there are human brains in the world, there can occur no human mental events.

Yet human brains seem *par excellence* to be entities that can survive some alterations and cannot survive others; they seem to have essential properties, properties they must retain if they are to go on existing at all. Just what are those essential properties—to what natural kind do human brains belong? In chapter 7 I will present reasons for thinking that human brains all by themselves amount to a particular natural kind. But even there I will defend only general remarks about the *kinds* of properties that characterize them essentially. Specific answers on the properties essential to human brains is a question for empirical science, I will argue. Still it is safe to say that human brains must retain certain properties of structure and organization if they are to go on existing at all. A human brain cannot survive being compressed to the size of a sugar cube; it will likewise be destroyed if a bolt of lightning vaporizes it and disperses its component molecules. If human brains exist in the world at all, there exist in the world entities that essentially have a certain structure and organization.

Suppose then that some human brain undergoes a change that removes some of these properties of structure. In virtue of what is this change a destruction—an end of an existence—rather than merely an alteration in something that continues to exist? Conventionalists—at least, conventionalists who believe there are in the world objects—must answer: in virtue of our having the conventions of individuation that we have. But our having our conventions is a matter of our thinking and talking in certain ways. It is a matter of our undergoing certain mental events. So the occurrence in the world of at least some human mental events is logically prior to the existence in the world of human brains. For it is in virtue of our conventions that there are in the world entities having essentially the properties of structure that human brains have essentially.

Thus conventionalists who are materialists must say: the existence in the world of human brains is logically prior to the occurrence in the world of human mental events, and the occurrence in the world of human mental events is logically prior to the existence in the world of human brains. This is a paradox.[4] And by "paradox" I do not mean a pleasant puzzle about which to spin articles. It is a paradox in the original sense—it is *para doxa*, beyond belief.

Can conventionalists who believe that there are in the world objects—conventionalists who eschew Sidelle's austerely realist picture—save themselves by embracing dualism? But even dualists must claim that there are certain changes that human minds can survive, and others that they cannot. A human mind can pass from entertaining one thought to entertaining another without ceasing to exist. But a human mind cannot acquire an atomic number of 79 or a valence of +3. If there suddenly arises, where a moment ago there was found a human mind, an entity having atomic number 79, then there a human mind has ceased to exist—surely even a dualist must agree with this. But in virtue of what is a change in the thought entertained merely an alteration in a human mind—merely a switch in properties accidental to a human mind—while drastic alterations like the one just considered amount to the ending of a human mind's existence? Conventionalists who are dualists must answer: in virtue of our having the conventions of individuation that we have. So the occurrence in the world of human mental events is again logically prior to the existence of human minds. But isn't the occurrence of human mental events logically posterior to the existence of minds that can undergo them? I shall assume that any dualist must answer Yes—that any dualist must deny that mental events can occur logically prior to, and independently of, the existence in the world of minds.

But then *any* conventionalist who believes that there are in the world objects—any conventionalist electing the anti-realist picture—is caught in a paradox.

What then of Sidelle's austerely realist picture of the world? Here there are no objects, no courses of existence, no distinctions between mere alterations and outright destructions (or creations). There is only world-stuff, on the one hand, and on the other hand us and our conventions of individuation.

But let us ask: why are the conventions of ours, in virtue of which some properties of the objects which we believe in are essential, and other properties merely accidental, called "conventions *of individuation*"? Because there is a close connection between our individuating as we do and our affirming the modal judgements that we affirm. Thus far we have observed this connection only at the level of kinds. We have noted that, for Sidelle, our conventions forbid us to classify any substance envisioned in some imagined world as being "the same chemical stuff" as the water with which we are familiar unless we are prepared to think of that substance as sharing the same microstructure that familiar water has. We sense that this is our convention, and articulate the awareness by asserting that water takes microstructure H_2O with it through all possible worlds—that water essentially has that microstructure—since we incautiously suppose that *there is* in the world water, and other stuffs such as water, and thereby are required to suppose that there are in the world necessities.

But the connection between individuation and modal commitments obtains at the level of individual objects and samples as well. In order to judge that there exist, at the same time, *two* individual Ks, we must believe that there exists at that time a K having some property p, and a K having some property p', such that no one K *can* simultaneously have p and p'. The clearest example of such thinking involves spatial locations. We typically are prepared to judge that there *now* exist in the world two objects of a space-taking sort O if and only if we suppose that there now exists an O having spatial location s, and an O having location s', such that no one O can at a time have both s and s'. And it is in general easy to suppose this: with rare and strange exceptions, we suppose that extended objects of any kind necessarily cannot simultaneously occupy two discontinuous spatial regions. Almost as familiar are examples of analogous thinking involving temporal locations. Might there *here* exist, over the course of the world's history, two distinct individual Ts—two entities of a kind that enjoys temporally extended existence? With rare and strange exceptions, it is a sufficient condition for our judging this that we suppose there here exists, over history, a *T* having a career that spans certain times, and a *T* having a career that spans other times, such that no one *T* can exist across both spans. And supposing this is at least often necessary for our judging there here to exist over history two *Ts*. To suppose this is typically easy: almost without exception, we suppose that no time-taking object can exist across temporally discontinuous spans of time. In the cases where we need *not* be persuaded of such temporal discontinuity, to judge that there here exist over history two distinct *Ts*, that will be because we suppose the *T* existing here at the later time had some one property, and the *T* existing here at the earlier time had some other property, such that no *T* can over its lifespan have both.

But the point is wholly general, and applies even to entities not located in space and time. We treat it as a necessary and sufficient condition, for there to exist in the world two (or more) *Xs*, that there exist in the world an *X* having some property *p*, and an *X* having some property *p'* (etc.), such that no one *X* *can* have both *p* and *p'*. Joint possession of *p* and *p'* must be impossible for *Xs*—it must be something that *Xs* by nature cannot do, something incompatible with what *Xs* essentially are like. The occurrence of a plurality of individuals of the same type, our conventions of individuation say, involves the obtaining of incompatibilities-with-some-essential-nature.

But the worldview Sidelle offers us holds that it is by virtue of our existing, and having the practices of individuation that we do, that there appear to be in the world any necessities and any essences—and that appearance is, moreover, deceptive. It seems fair to ask: in virtue of what are we a "we"—a plurality of minds—and in virtue of what are our conventions of individuation plural? Is there nonconventional or preconventional individuation in the world? If so, our conventions of individuation are not the sole ground of "necessities," and necessities are not mere appearances. If not, the obtaining in the world of our conventions of individuation is logically prior to the existence of *us* as a plurality—and for that matter is logically prior to the conventions' being *conventions*, plural. Yet surely it must *also* be true that our *existing* in the world is logically prior to our having any particular conventions.

I conclude that even Sidelle's version of the conventionalist position is *para doxa*—beyond belief.

1.4 Lewis-style Conventionalism

Before closing this section, and while we are still on the topic of plurality and individuation, I will comment briefly on a variant of conventionalism that holds that there are different correct answers, depending on the conversational context, as to which properties, or which *sorts* of properties, are essential to a given stuff or kind or individual. This is David Lewis's "counterpart theory" about essential properties (Lewis 1986b, pp. 248–263). Lewis holds, as is well known, that there are countless real worlds in addition to the actual world. Hence any individual object in the actual world is significantly similar, in one respect or several, to countless nonactual objects across this range of worlds. The samples of any actual stuff, the members of any actual kind, will likewise all be similar to countless sets of otherworldly samples or otherworldly kind-mates. So we have in principle a great deal of latitude as to *which* otherworldly objects we will treat as *counterparts* to a given individual object or kind or stuff—as truthmakers for statements about ways the given object or kind or stuff could possibly be, even though

it is not actually that way. Yet the interests and presupposi-
tions we bring with us, to any given conversational context,
will limit what can count there as counterparts. "Two things
may be counterparts in one context, but not in another; or it
may be indeterminate whether two things are counterparts"
(1986b, p. 254). The right thing to say, about which of the
properties of an individual or kind or stuff are essential to
it, will then be just as shifting, as subject to indeterminacy,
and as context sensitive as is the extension of the counterpart relation. If a property possessed by a given individual
or kind is missing in some of the contextually relevant counterparts, that property is accidental to the individual or
kind; if the property is possessed by all relevant counterparts, that property is essential. In different contexts, different answers will be correct as to which properties are
essential and which are accidental.

It takes a moment to understand just what this view of
Lewis's is a view *about*. Is it a view about what it is for properties to be essential to an individual or a kind or a stuff? On
the traditional conception, the properties essential to an individual are properties it is by nature incapable of losing; those
essential to a kind or a stuff are properties that any member
of that kind, any sample of that stuff, is by nature incapable
of lacking. Can it happen that an individual or kind or stuff
should lack any of the properties which it is by nature incapable of lacking? No, that is a contradiction in terms. Can it
happen that a given individual or kind should be or become
capable of lacking properties that it by nature is incapable of
lacking? No, that too is a contradiction in terms.

So any theory that says that the properties essential to a
given individual or kind differ, relative to different contexts,
is not a theory about what it is for properties to be *essential*
at all. I infer that Lewis's view is *not* about what it is for

properties to be essential, and that Lewis does not believe that, strictly, objects have any properties essentially. No, the real topic of Lewis's view must be what I suggested at the outset: it is a theory about correctly *saying* which properties are and are not essential to a given individual or kind or stuff. Our *saying* that these and those properties are essential to this or that individual or kind has to be the root phenomenon, on Lewis's view. A given property's *being* essential to this or that individual or kind has to be merely the flickering shadow, the inconstant projection, of the sayings that are required of us, in the conversational context, by our interests and customs and conventions. The latter render certain attributions of essential status *correct*. But no such attribution is ever literally *true*.

Lewis's view then is a variant of conventionalism, a projectivist view about essential status. Should we think of it as reflecting an austere ontology, like Sidelle's, on which there are only our sayings and a neutral world-stuff? Or should we think of it as an antirealist view, on which there are objects in the world, but projected objects, objects whose careers we construct? Lewis's texts comport better with the latter interpretation, but there are difficulties, as we have seen, with either alternative. Yet there are additional difficulties for Lewis, I suggest, connected with the very claim that there is a *plurality* of conversational contexts. The contexts evidently are plural independently, and prior to, the being-correct of *any* attributions of essential status. It is fair then to ask: in virtue of what are the contexts *contexts*, in the plural; what constitutes their distinctness from one another? If conversational contexts were distinct from one another in virtue of bare haecceities alone, it could not be explained how we learn which conventions and practices apply in *this* context, and which others apply in *that* context. The contexts must then be qualitatively different from one another. The distinctness of context C_1 from context C_2 must rest on the fact that property p_1 is somehow involved in C_1, property p_2 is involved in place of p_1 in C_2, and p_1 and p_2 exclude one another—no single context can feature p_1 and p_2 in just the same role. But the only way of spelling out "in place of" or "in the same role as" is to identify property bearers common to C_1 and C_2, property bearers that can have p_1 and can have p_2 but cannot, while remaining themselves, have both p_1 and p_2. This certainly seems to make the distinctness from one another, of distinct conversational contexts, logically posterior to the difference, in the case of these property bearers, between their accidental and their essential properties. But if so, essential status cannot be *merely* the projection of what it is correct to say in the various conversational contexts.

1.5   Escape from Paradox

Conventionalism, I contend, ultimately founders on its refusal to allow that any objects in the world possess mind-independent existences. On pain of paradox we must allow that at least human minds themselves have mind-independent existences. Almost certainly we must also allow that human brains and bodies have mind-independent existences, and that the various material objects with which we interact have such existences as well.

But to make out these claims we must hold that the essential*ness* of the properties essential to nature's kinds is independent of us—not a status for which we are responsible. And this returns us to the epistemological question: how do we manage to detect the essentialness of nature's essential properties?

2   The Epistemology of Real Natures

Conventionalism, I have argued, fails to give a believable explanation of how we come by our knowledge of properties essential to nature's kinds and stuffs and phenomena. And we do seem to have such knowledge. We know that gold necessarily has atomic number 79, that snow flakes by nature have symmetrical shapes, and that lightning is essentially an electrical phenomenon. To give examples just slightly more controversial, we know that hearts by nature have the function of pumping blood (see chapter 7) and that people by nature are organisms (see chapter 8).

Is the essential status that we know some properties to have, for one or another of nature's kinds, a status that they possess independently of us? In the previous chapter I argued that objects that have mind-independent existences—careers that begin and end at particular points, independently of how we think about those objects—must have essential properties whose status as essential is mind-independent. And everyone, I argued, must concede that at least some objects or entities have mind-independent existences. Proponents of even the most antirealist ontologies must assign mind-independent existences at least to minds and to elements of their physical or cultural surroundings.

A great many philosophers—perhaps most—are of course inclined to credit vastly more objects with mind-independent existences.

But then the question of how we can *know* certain properties to be essential to the objects belonging to this or that natural kind—or to the samples of a given natural stuff, or the instances of a given natural phenomenon—appears truly imposing. If objects are out there, tracing out mind-independent existences, surely one wants to allow that at least sometimes we can know *which* properties are essential to them—which properties it is, the disappearance of which marks the ends of their existences. But if we can sometimes know that certain properties have essential status, and if essential status is out there in the world rather than bestowed by us, how do we learn of it from the world? It is easy enough to see how we establish by induction that all samples of gold *are* composed of atoms having 79 protons in their nucleus. But how can we discover that samples of *that stuff*, of gold, *must* be so composed, *by nature* are so composed?

In this chapter I argue that there is an empirical test for essentialness that we do, and should, commonly rely on. That we do have such a test in our repertoire may seem an astonishing claim, given that most philosophers have for 220 years agreed with Kant that "experience tells us, indeed, what is, but not that it must necessarily be so" (Kant 1929, p. 42). But the explanation is simple. The test is one we run in several steps. No individual step is adequate to warrant a conclusion of essentialness. What has been overlooked is that a number of such steps together constitute a single, if protracted, test of essentialness.

Why has this been overlooked? I hazard this surmise: over the past 220 years philosophers have largely overlooked the importance, stressed by Hegel and by Aristotle before him, of contrariety.[1] Any property's identity consists in—or at least crucially involves—its contrasting, to varying degrees, with its own proper contraries. That at least is what I shall argue in this chapter. If this starting premise is true, it follows that testing for essentialness is a multistepped affair. First, we must establish that Ks are in fact uniformly characterized by properties in a certain cluster—say, by properties f, g, and h. Subsequently, we must discover that items generically akin to Ks, and differing from Ks by bearing some property (say, f') contrary to a property that Ks uniformly have, likewise uniformly bear properties contrary to others of the properties Ks uniformly have (the generically similar kind will have, say, g' and h'). I call this "the test of flanking uniformities." It is the test which—without quite realizing it—we do rely on for judging that Ks have f essentially. Because the starting premise is, as I shall argue, true—because any property's identity involves its contrasting with its own proper contraries—it is the test we should rely on.

2.1 Why Suppose That Essential Properties Occur in Clusters?

But in order to establish this position I must first address a simpler question: why suppose that essential properties need occur in clusters at all? Why might there not be natural kinds whose members are essentially characterized by just a single essential property? Philosophers who hold that essential status is mind-dependent can answer: "well, the only natural kinds that it is useful for us to recognize—the only ones about which we can come to make informative inferences—are ones characterized by multifaceted essential natures; indeed Mill had a point in thinking of natural kinds as characterized by *indefinitely* rich essential natures."[2] But if essentialness is fixed not by our interests and classificatory practices, but by the way the world is, this answer fails to show that there might not *be* natural kinds, uninteresting to us, whose members were essentially characterized by just one property.

To answer this question I shall help myself to the assumption that all essential properties do have contrasting contraries; defense of this assumption will come in 2.3 and 2.4, where I will argue that any property must have contrasting contraries, since its very identity crucially involves its contrasting with them. Thus *having atomic number 79* contrasts with *having atomic number 80*, and more sharply contrasts with *having atomic number 19*; *having just that lattice structure*, as said of quartz crystals, contrasts with *having the arrangement of molecules in diamonds or in glass*.

Suppose then that the members of natural kind *K*—*K*s— are essentially characterized *at least* by property *f*, which contrasts with contrary properties *f′* and *f″*. Can it be argued that *K*s must essentially be characterized by other properties as well? The first step is to ask what is added, to the idea that *K*s in fact have *f* uniformly, by the claim that *K*s have *f* essentially. That *K*s in fact uniformly have *f* entails that no *K* in fact bears *f′* or *f″*. That *K*s have *f* essentially, necessarily, entails that *K*s are *incapable* of having *f′* or *f″*. So we can know of any further object we discover that does have *f′* or *f″*—however great the similarity obtaining between that object and *K*s themselves—that that object is different in kind from *K*s themselves.

But now just what is this that we know of such an object? Just what do we infer, from the premise that this object differs by virtue of *f′* or *f″* from *K*s, when we draw the conclusion that this object belongs to a different natural kind from *K*s? Not *just* that this object has *f'* rather than *f*—that is the premise of our inference, not its conclusion. Rather we infer some further or other separateness of this object from all *K*s, some further exclusion of this object from the natural kind *K*. But kinds are individuated by their characterizing properties. So we infer some further or other *qualitative* difference between this object and *K*s. We infer that this object differs from *K*s not just in lacking *f* but in lacking some further property—or properties, plural—which *K*s all have. It is (in part) in the lacking of these further properties that the differing-in-natural-kind consists. So it is in the *possessing* of these further properties that *K*s' *belonging* to their own natural kind in part consists. These further properties are further *essential* properties.

2.2   What Holds Together the Properties in an Essential Nature?

So whether (as I deny) essentialness is mind bestowed, or instead is mind independent, the same holds true: essential properties by nature occur in clusters or packages. Where the properties in such a package come jointly to be instanced, there does an existence begin; where joint instantiation of the properties ceases, there does an existence end.

But the next important question is how, if at all, the properties in such a cluster are held together. Do all the properties in such a cluster crop up, in member after member of a given natural kind, because of the way the world works? Or do the world's workings leave it possible for one or several properties in such a package to disappear, even where all the rest remain jointly instanced? In the latter case the properties in such a package will "hold together" only in the

sense that *we* are unwilling to *allow* that a member of the
natural kind in question can have neither quite ceased to
exist nor cleanly continued to exist either. The properties
will hold together, across members of the natural kind, only
in the sense—and to the extent—that we refuse to classify
something as *belonging* to that natural kind unless it presents
the *full* complement of properties in the package.

But this latter answer seems to put us in the position of
constructing the existences of the world's objects, just as
surely as if we were responsible for the essentialness of their
essential properties taken one by one. I shall take the arguments of the previous chapter as showing that such a position is not in general tenable.

The answer we must rather give, then, is that the properties composing an essential nature are held together by
virtue of the laws of nature (more on this in 2.6). By virtue
of these laws, some such properties individually, or several
in combination, will ground the presence of other such
properties. Turning the same point around, individual properties in an essential nature will, by virtue of the laws of
nature, be necessary conditions for other properties in that
nature—either for some one other property individually, or
for one-or-another of several other properties.

But need there be—as the recent fixation on gold and
water as sample natural kinds has suggested—some *single*
property in each essential nature that somehow is responsible for the presence of *all* the rest? There is no warrant
for thinking so, at least none provided by the traditional
concept of a natural kind. Traditionally, a natural kind is a
family of items over which attentive inductions will nonac-
cidentally turn out to be true—a family united by a common
essential nature, not found among items outside the family.
(That is why the basis of the induction must be an *attentive*

inspection of members *of the kind in question*.) So members of each natural kind must be characterized essentially by properties that, at least *in combination*, are found among members of no other kind. But need there be, for each natural kind, some one property that individually is found in members of no other kind? That *would* follow if each essential nature had to incorporate some one property which underlies, is responsible for, all the rest. But that requirement is unmotivated. All that is required by the traditional conception is that each essential nature incorporate enough properties to ensure a combination found in no other kind. The properties which do the underlying may be plural in number. They may be, individually, fairly indistinctive and run-of-the-mill. All that is required is that *in combination* they ensure, by virtue of the laws of nature, a package found in no other natural kind.

2.3   Contrast with Contraries as Crucial to Any Property's Identity

The idea that the properties in any essential nature are held together by the world—and hence incorporate some properties whose presence is a necessary condition for the presence of other properties in that nature—is the relatively uncontroversial premise in the argument that essentialness is empirically detectable via "the test of flanking uniformities." The more controversial premise is that any property's very identity is tied to its place in a range of contraries. The first premise entails that any essential nature is the subject of a counterfactual truth: that if such-and-such properties in a given essential nature were absent in a roughly similar essential nature, certain other properties in the given nature would be absent as well. The second premise casts light on what it is for a given property to be absent from an essential nature. For it tells us what the obtaining of that property amounts to or involves. In this section and the next I argue for the second premise.

But first a word on what contrariety is—on what gathers together the properties in a given contrary range. Contrariety involves incompatibility, but something more as well. To put it roughly at first, a property's contraries are its own proper rivals, relevant alternatives to that property, properties in some way akin to the given property. Thus *having atomic number 79* is incompatible with *having atomic number 66*, but no less is incompatible with *having IQ 134*—since atoms lack the cognitive capacities that are measured by IQ tests—and yet only the former of these is a property contrary to *having atomic number 79. Having a normal body temperature of 98.6°* is incompatible both with *having a normal body temperature of 97.6°* and with *having valence +3*, but only the former is a contrary.

But can the intuitive idea of "proper rivalry" be made more precise? John Bigelow and Robert Pargetter (1990, pp. 53–62) have shown that it can. What connects any property with all and only its true contraries is that any property will differ from its own contraries to differing degrees— differing, but commensurable. To have atomic number 79 is to differ from anything that has atomic number 70, and to differ more sharply from anything that has atomic number 16, and less sharply from anything having atomic number 78. But the difference bestowed on a thing by its having atomic number 79 from anything having IQ 134 is not *more* sharp or *less* sharp than any of those differences; it is a complete lack of connection, not commensurable with any of that thing's differences from things characterized by truly contrary properties.

My contention then is that any property's being the property it is consists at least partly in its contrasting, to the various (but commensurable) degrees it does, with its own proper contraries. Or, to put it differently, the contention is that what it is for objects to *have* any given property is, at least in part, for those objects to *differ* to varying (but commensurable) degrees from all and any objects that bear particular *other* properties. How might one argue for this position? In fact the first step is to identify reasons why an argument might be needed—reasons a person might have for resisting the position. After all it seems at first blush undeniable that for an object to have the property of weighing 3.2 kg is, at least largely, for it to differ just slightly from any objects weighing 3.4 kg or 3.0 kg, to differ more from any objects weighing 8.0 kg, and so on. Assuming *arguendo* that there are such properties as colors—as the literature on contrariety has assumed (following Wittgenstein 1929), although the claim is in fact questionable (Clark 2000, ch. 6)—it seems very much a part of something's being red that it differs just slightly from anything orange but quite markedly from anything purple, and so forth.

Historically the resistance has derived from allegiance to an atomistic ontology. The thought has been that the obtaining in the world of any one property should not in and of itself amount to the obtaining of any other. This thought can, I think, more perspicuously be expressed if we speak of properties as ways-for-things-to-be. Then the motive for resistance is this thought: that there is in the world *this* way-for-things-to-be does not in itself amount to there being in the world any *other* ways-for-things-to-be. Properties stand on their own two feet, ontologically; they are not propped into existence by leaning on—more accurately, by pushing against—one another.

But such atomism about properties has historically been confronted by embarrassing questions about the relations of incompatibility and contrast that obtain between contrary properties. There is a fairly drastic response to these questions discernible in Leibniz, and a subtle response offered by David Armstrong. I now shall contend that neither of these responses is acceptable. This will amount to an argument that we should reject the atomism which compels us to choose between these responses. Thereby it will amount to an argument that we have no reason *not* to agree that contrast-with-contraries is central to any property's identity.

But first, the embarrassing questions themselves. Suppose then that in addition to the way-for-things-to-be that is the property of *weighing 3.2 kg*, there in fact is also in the world the way-for-things-to-be that is the property of *weighing 28 kg*. The atomist viewpoint says: what it is for there to be in the world the first way-of-being does not in itself amount to there obtaining in the world any relations of contrast or exclusion with other ways-of-being; and likewise with the second way-of-being. But *weighing 3.2 kg* in fact does exclude *weighing 28 kg*, and indeed contrasts with the latter rather sharply. Even atomists must admit that these relations of incompatibility and contrast really obtain in the world. But they must consider them to be *extrinsic* to the very *being*, the identities, of the properties which stand in them. This in turn seems to suggest that these relations obtain contingently, not necessarily. For it seems we must reason thus: so far as *there being* in the world *weighing 3.2 kg* goes—even so far as there being *weighing 3.2 kg* and there being *weighing 28 kg* goes—there is so far no assurance or requirement of any specific relations of incompatibility or contrast. Those relations are an extra, not ensured by the world's being populated (in part) by those properties. So those relations are contingent—but surely this is an embarrassing result. It seems utterly unbelievable that weighing 3.2 kg might have been compatible with weighing 28 kg, or that it might have been only slightly different from weighing 28 kg. Could *red* conceivably have been quite similar to *green*?

How might an atomist respond? The response which some interpreters see in Leibniz is to bite the bullet of contingency (Millikan 1984, p. 269; cf. Adams 1995, pp. 393–394). In themselves any two properties are compossible; if in fact two properties cannot be coinstantiated, that is because some external agent, namely God, made it impossible for them to be coinstantiated. (Just how God managed to do this, and whether He could or might subsequently unmake the impossibility, are questions better left unaddressed.) But is it really believable that in the absence of divine interference, *being red* could have been compatible with *being green*? I have no actual argument to offer against this suggestion; I simply cannot see how one can entertain it in the first place.

2.4   An Objection: Armstrong's Atomistic Picture of Properties

David Armstrong offers a far more subtle response. On Armstrong's view, the fact that there are in the world *weighing 3.2 kg* and *weighing 28 kg does* all by itself ensure that there obtain the relations of incompatibility and contrast we have noted; yet the *being* of these properties, or of any other properties—their identity—lies strictly in their being intrinsically just *this* way-of-being, not in their contrasting with any other ways-of-being. Armstrong's picture of properties is atomistic.

Here is how Armstrong articulates this position. All the properties in any range of contraries (or all but one) are, Armstrong holds, complex properties or "structural universals" (Armstrong 1978, pp. 120–129; 1988). What it is for something to have f, say, is for it to comprise a proper part that has property P_1, another proper part that has P_2, and a third that has P_3. The other properties in f's range are related to f by "partial identity." Thus to have f', say, is to comprise just two proper parts, one having P_1 and one having P_2. The incompatibility of contraries then reduces to the trivial impossibility—acceptable even to atomists—that anything, including any property, should be something other than itself. Suppose first—to see the point most easily—that one of the contraries of f is a simple property f''. Having f'' then amounts in effect to comprising a part that has P_1, and no other part. (That is, roughly, f''-ness just is P_1-ness.) But then *of course* nothing that has f can have f''; having f is comprising a part having P_1 *together with other parts*. Yet the impossibility is only a trivial one. And the same trivial impossibility prevents anything that has f' from having f. It does not matter if *all* the properties in a contrary range are complex, so long as they overlap in the right way.

Such an analysis works admirably for the contrariety of such properties as weighing 5 pounds and weighing 3 pounds, or being 4 feet long versus being 3 feet long, or lasting 10 minutes versus lasting 2. It even works, as Armstrong has recently shown, for contraries such as being triangular versus being quadrilateral versus being pentagonal, or such as an angle's being right versus acute versus obtuse (Armstrong 1997, pp. 55–56).

But what if there are properties that objects have only as wholes—without their parts having weakened or partial versions of them? Supposing that there are such properties is just supposing that some aggregations (or heaps) of parts may amount to wholes in nature, and not just relative to our classificatory practices. Examples might include having a valence of +3, developing a maximum horsepower of 409, or having degree of stability n, as said in population genetics of a particular combination of genes.

Say then that some internal combustion engine develops a maximum horsepower of 409. Then it may well comprise a proper part that would develop a lesser horsepower; perhaps if four of the eight cylinders were lopped off, the resulting engine would produce 150 hp. But the problem for Armstrong's position is that *all* the incompatibilities between properties in a given contrary range are to be explained by appeal to partial identities. Consider then the incompatibility between developing 409 hp at the maximum and developing just 407. Armstrong's explanation must be that what it is for something to have a maximum hp of 409 is for it to comprise a part that develops a maximum of 407 *together with another part* that adds yet more—specifically, 2 hp more. But it seems impossible to discern, within a 409 hp engine, a proper part that develops 407. If some proper part truly were in its own right responsible for 407 hp, it would have to be able to develop 407 hp all by itself—that is, if separated off from the original engine. But the smallest removal of a part from the 409 engine that affects its power at all reduces it to far less than 407. It is even harder to discern, within the 409 engine, the bit responsible for the extra 2 hp, and for exactly the same reason.

The valence of an element, as originally conceived, concerns the disposition of its atoms to bond with other atoms. Strictly speaking the different valences are incompatible with one another only over the lighter elements, namely, up through scandium on the periodic table; heavier elements (e.g., iron) can have more than one valence (e.g., can bond in either the valence +2 or the valence +3 way). Still, even the heavier elements have only one maximally stable way of bonding, one maximally stable valence. So *maximally stable valences* are true contraries. If some atom has a (maximally stable) valence of +3, does it comprise a proper part that has a (maximally stable) valence of +2, and also a proper part that has a valence of +1? Not as a rule. A proper part that had in its own right a valence of +2 or +1 would have to take that valence with it when existing on its own. Yet some ways of breaking pieces off an atom can yield atoms having *higher* valence. Abstractly, indeed, this can happen in innumerable ways: just move up one row in the periodic table from the original atom, then move right for a proper part having higher positive valence, left for a proper part having higher negative valence. But separation of a higher-valence proper part does also happen in nature.[3] And while it is true that valence has come to be understood in a nondispositional way, with the development of atomic theory, the current understanding is of no help to Armstrong. Valence is now seen as the number of gaps in the outermost electron shell. But the problem here, for the "partial identity" view, is that electron shells do not in any clear sense have parts. If an outermost electron shell has three gaps, it does not follow that some part of that shell has two gaps.

Finally, consider a combination of genes that population genetics determines to have degree of stability n. That combination has a degree of stability that contrasts with, and is incompatible with, some lesser degree of stability m. Armstrong's position says these relations of contrast and incompatibility obtain in virtue of the fact that anything with degree of stability n comprises a proper part that itself has degree of stability m, together with yet another proper part. But commonly this is just not true. Commonly a combination of genes comprises genes that individually have a higher degree of stability than the combination itself.

An atomist about properties, persuaded that Armstrong has pointed the way to an escape from the embarrassing questions about incompatibility among contraries, might insist that there really is no such property as horsepower, or even no such property as valence. But it would be implausible to claim that there are no properties at all that objects have only as wholes—without the parts having reduced versions of them. Indeed there seem to be many such properties. So there seem to be many properties for which atomism is untenable—properties for which contrariety is a self-standing phenomenon, not reducible to the intrinsic being of the properties involved. But if atomism is not defensible for *all* properties, just on account of their *being* properties, then there is no reason not to agree with my second main premise. The very being, the identity, of any property consists at least in part in its contrasting as it does with its own proper contraries.

2.5   The Test of Flanking Uniformities

Let us now return to the result established in 2.2: any essential nature includes some properties such that, were they to be absent in a roughly similar essential nature, certain other properties in the original nature would have to be absent as well. And now let f be such a property in the essential nature of Ks. Just what is involved in f's being absent from the essential nature of another kind roughly similar to Ks? Begin with what is involved in f's being *present* in the essential nature of Ks, on the view advocated in the previous two sections. This is for Ks to contrast with any and all items bearing a range of other properties, say f', f'', and f'''—with some of them sharply, with others just mildly, but with items bearing each of these other properties to a unique and determinate degree. So for f to be *absent* from the essential nature of a roughly similar natural kind will be for there to be a *failure* of contrast with one of these groups—with items bearing f', or else items bearing f'', and so on. Or, to put it differently, it will be for items bearing this roughly similar essential nature—members of this roughly similar natural kind—to contrast with Ks themselves. But such contrasting by nature occurs to one determinate degree or another. So the absence of f, from an essential nature roughly similar to Ks', is never an undifferentiated, yes-or-no matter. It is a departure to one degree or another, by items bearing that roughly similar essential nature, from the f-ness present in Ks.

But the idea put forth in 2.2 is that f's absence, in an essential nature roughly similar to that of Ks, must go together with the absence there of some other property (say, g) likewise present in the nature of Ks, because f is tacked onto g by the way the world works. The world itself is such that the presence of g ensures the presence of f. So if the absence of f in any roughly similar essential nature is really a matter of degree—a matter of greater or lesser departure from f-ness—the corresponding absence of g in such a nature, engineered by the way the world works, must be a matter of *corresponding* degree. It must be a matter of the bearers of this roughly similar essential nature departing, to a corresponding and commensurate degree, from the g-ness of Ks.

In other words: members of any natural kind generically similar to Ks, essentially characterized by some property f^* contrary to f, instead of by f itself, will likewise be characterized, uniformly, by some one contrary of g—a contrary g^*

that contrasts as sharply with g as f^* does with f. This follows from the premise that f is a property whose presence in the essential nature of Ks is ensured—required—by other properties (in this example, g alone) in the essential nature of Ks. But *any* essential nature, 2.2 argued, will incorporate some properties ensured or required by others (individually, or in combination) in the nature.

It follows that there is an empirical test for essentialness. To gain evidence that f characterizes Ks not just uniformly but essentially, see whether, among the members of (what seem to be) natural kinds roughly similar to Ks, differing from Ks by possessing some one property or another contrary to f, there are uniformly found *other* properties contrasting with *other* properties uniformly possessed by Ks. In the simple case we have been considering—where the presence of f in the nature of Ks is ensured by the presence there of g alone—one would expect to find, among all members of similar kinds characterized by one contrary or another of f, uniform presence of a contrary of g *commensurately* contrasting with g itself. But more complex cases are common. Commonly, that is, the presence of a given property f in the essential nature of a given kind K will be produced by the presence in that nature of a *combination* of other properties. So departures from f, in the natures of natural kinds roughly similar to Ks, may not be accompanied by other properties that *individually* contrast to an exactly *commensurate* degree with other individual properties of Ks.

But this much remains true. If f is an essential property of Ks, then other kinds similar to Ks, characterized uniformly by one contrary of f or another, will each differ in just one uniform way from *other* properties found uniformly among Ks: the similar kinds will each select, throughout their membership, just some one contrary of another property, or of each of several other properties, found uniformly among *K*s. That is "the test of flanking uniformities."

Thus it is warranted to judge that atomic number 79 is an essential property of gold because other physical elements, each characterized by one atomic number contrary to atomic number 79, also differ, always in the same way, from *other* properties found always in gold. Other metals select in all samples a particular melting point contrary to gold's melting point, a particular specific gravity contrary to gold's specific gravity, and so on. It is warranted to judge that quartz crystals *essentially* have a certain lattice arrangement among their molecules because other mineral formations, each characterized by a different molecular arrangement, likewise are characterized in all their instances by just some one contrary of other properties of quartz—by just some one scratch index, just some one density, just some one color, and so forth.

The test of flanking uniformities thus yields conclusions about the properties essential to nature's kinds and stuffs and phenomena strictly from what we learn from experience. It does not require that we know independently of experience—via a priori insight, or via armchair expression of our conventions of individuation—"template" truths about the kinds of kinds (physical elements, mineral formations, chemical compounds, etc.) into which nature's specific kinds fall. Rather it shows how we may *learn* such truths from experience. It shows how we may first establish that *this* chemical compound we call "water" has a certain molecular structure essentially, that *that* generically similar stuff we call "alcohol" has a contrary molecular structure essentially, that such-and-such an "acid" has yet another molecular structure essentially, and can then perform a metainduction over chemical compounds, thus establishing that each has essentially whatever the molecular structure that observation determines it to have. Our observation of nature does indeed have to be supplemented by good luck, if not by nonempirical knowledge, in order for the test of flanking uniformities to yield conclusions. We must be lucky enough to find kinds generically similar to Ks, and smart enough to recognize them as being generically similar, in order for the test to teach us anything about Ks' essential properties. But most of the ways of learning about the world we wield are like that. They will not invariably yield the kind of knowledge that makes us favor them; they even may, in the short run, yield misleading conclusions which subsequent applications of them can correct. But only allegiance to verificationism can make us uneasy at the prospect that the ways the world is—including the ways the world must be—may outrun our abilities to learn of them.

2.6   But What if Laws Governing Ks Fail to Hold in Worlds Containing Ks?

But there is an objection to what I have said in 2.2—an objection that will by now have been bothering some readers for a long time. It runs this way: "The members of any natural kind K must retain all their truly essential properties in all possible worlds. But then the essential properties of Ks cannot include some (e.g., f) that are cemented to others (e.g., g) by merely the laws of nature. For the actual laws of nature fail to obtain in some possible worlds. In particular, the laws actually bearing on Ks fail to obtain in some possible worlds in which Ks themselves are present. So there are possible worlds in which there really are Ks, but the Ks lack f. The test of flanking uniformities may *say* that f is an essential property of Ks, but so much the worse for that test."

The reasoning behind this objection runs as follows. "We can imagine possible worlds in which items answering to our concept of Ks occur, but in which the laws of nature are different from what they actually are. In particular we can imagine worlds in which such items bear g—and let us say that the bearing of g *is* written in to our concept of Ks—but lack f. So there are possible worlds in which Ks lack f. The property f is not a truly essential property of Ks."

The outlines of the response I offer to this reasoning have been familiar for thirty years (see Kripke 1972; cf. Elder 1994). I deny that in imagining such worlds we are imagining worlds truly containing Ks, rather than mere look-alikes. Or, if it is open to my opponent to *stipulate* that the worlds he is imagining are worlds containing Ks, I deny that the worlds my opponent envisages are *possible* worlds.

After all, how is my opponent so sure that the worlds he imagines are truly possible worlds, truly containing Ks themselves? His confidence must trace to this thought: the concepts we in fact employ, for tracing the world's kinds and stuffs across the contexts and circumstances we in fact confront in our actual cognitive activities, spotlight properties that those kinds bear not just in all actual circumstances but even in all possible circumstances. Indeed our concepts manage to spotlight *all* the properties that nature's kinds and stuffs take with them through all possible circumstances. If our concept of Ks has the bearing of property g written right into it, but not the bearing of f, then Ks themselves—veritable Ks—are present in possible worlds in which they lack f.

I suggest that this degree of confidence is reckless and wholly unrealistic. That it is unrealistic emerges if, following Ruth Millikan (2000, ch. 1), one thinks of our concepts as reidentification recipes for nature's kinds that we form by implementing naturally selected cognitive abilities (see below, chapter 8). Natural selection virtually never insists on infallibility in the capacities and devices it installs in its creatures. It does not even insist on infallibility in the real-world circumstances in which those capacities and devices in fact get selected, far less infallibility across all possible worlds, however nomologically remote. So there is absolutely no reason to suppose that reidentification recipes fashioned by naturally selected abilities will be recipes infallible across all possible worlds. They may even be recipes that fail in the actual world (Millikan 2000, ch. 4).

I contend then that realistically, we have good reason to suspect that Ks may have essential properties *not* spotlighted by our concept of Ks; indeed we should even suspect that some of the properties that *are* spotlighted by our concept of Ks are merely usefully widespread markers of Ks, but not properties that Ks possess absolutely *everywhere*, and certainly not properties that Ks are *bound to* possess.

It follows that we have no positive reason for assurance that it is truly Ks we are imagining—not, at least, Ks in truly *possible* worlds—when we imagine worlds in which items answering to *our concept* of Ks are present, but without some properties attached to Ks here in the actual world by the laws of nature. Indeed we can have no positive reason for assurance that the laws of nature in fact bearing on Ks fail to obtain in any possible worlds in which Ks truly are present. We have no positive reason for assurance that the laws of nature are less than "strong."

3   Real Essential Natures, or Merely Real Kinds?

A challenge to the test set forth in the previous chapter, called by me "the test of flanking uniformities," has recently been raised by Michael Rea: that test may not yield evidence of true essentialness at all (Rea 2002, p. 132–134). That a property passes this test *may* show, Rea says, that it is a necessary condition for membership in a particular natural kind—a necessary condition, and one member of a set of properties that jointly are sufficient for membership. But we still must ask: what happens when a bearer of such a property loses that property? Or if the loss of one such property can never occur as an isolated event—if I am right to hold that the properties in any essential nature are bound together by the way the world works—we must ask, what happens when an object bearing *all* the properties in a particular cluster, certified as an "essential nature" by the test of flanking uniformities, ceases to have *any* of those properties?

Does the object simply cease to exist altogether? That is what we must think if the properties lost are truly *essential* properties, in the traditional sense employed thus far in this book. The loss of any *essential* property must amount to the end of an existence. Or does the object simply pass from a phase in which it was a member of one natural kind, to a new phase in which it is differently configured? It is often *supposed* that kind-membership is a life-and-death matter for objects—that an object cannot depart from the natural kind to which it belongs, without ceasing to exist. But of course there are views on matter (and on change and on composition) that suggest that the very thing that one day bears the properties jointly sufficient for membership in a given natural kind can on another day, while still continuing to exist, bear different properties.

Nothing in the test of flanking uniformities, Rea says, shows that the objects bearing the properties it examines cannot manage still to exist, even upon loss of those properties (Rea 2002, p. 134). So nothing in that test ensures that the properties that pass it are truly *essential* properties, in the traditional sense. They may be merely necessary conditions for membership in a given natural kind.

To Rea's challenge against the test for essentialness I have proposed, I counterpose a challenge of my own. Just what is shown by the disappearance at some particular place of a package of properties certified by my test as composing an "essential nature"? Should we, as I claim, take this as showing that some existence has ended? Or is it a better interpretation of the data to suppose merely that some object (or objects—more in a moment) has undergone an alteration? Or are the two hypotheses perhaps tied, on ordinary scientific criteria for evaluating empirical hypotheses?

I argue in this chapter that on all ordinary criteria of scientific evaluation, the hypothesis that only some alteration has occurred, when from a particular place the properties sufficient for membership in a particular natural kind have vanished, is empirically bankrupt and worthless. The hypothesis that some existence has ended may not be *highly* predictive—it may tell us little more than that from now on, certain properties and behaviors are not going to be found at the place in question, perhaps also suggesting something about the circumstances in which we can expect other members of the natural kind in question to get destroyed— but it has *some* predictive and explanatory value, and so wins by default. The hypothesis that only an alteration has occurred has *no* value in whichever version we take it, though for different reasons in each case, or so I will argue. What really has happened when my test says, and common sense supposes, that some object has ceased to exist? On one version of the "just alteration" position, what has happened is just that physical simples that formerly were arranged *K*-wise (table-wise, quartz-crystal-wise, gold-atom-wise) have come to be arranged differently; on another, that the aggregate of microparticles that a moment ago composed the object has come to be differently deployed; on another, that the enduring lump of matter that formerly composed the object has now assumed a new form; on another, that a four-dimensional object comprising distinct aggregates of microparticles, each found where common sense thinks the object exists, has time-slices quite different from the earlier ones; on another, that a lump of prime matter (or Sidellian "world-stuff") has dropped certain properties and acquired different ones. But no version of this story has any merit at all as an empirical interpretation of the data, I argue.

This is not of course to deny that it is *sometimes* scientifically illuminating to judge that, where common sense supposes an object to have been destroyed, all that really has happened is that something else (or several somethings else, e.g., molecules arranged in a lattice) has assumed a new form. I place five ice cubes in a dish on the kitchen counter, and return two hours later to find the ice cubes gone, and only a pool of liquid in the dish. Science does teach, I think, that nothing has really been destroyed here—that all that has happened is that a particular sample of H_2O has passed from one molecular arrangement to another—even if precisely those words do not appear in the seventh-grade science book. For science teaches that water is H_2O, that ice is H_2O, and that steam is H_2O. But science does not of course teach that ice is steam. The explanation for this apparent inconsistency is (*pace* Mark Johnston 1997) that "water is H_2O" bespeaks a theoretical reduction that, like most theoretical reductions, jettisons *some* of what is claimed by the theory being reduced. "Folk physics" evidently claims that when a cube of ice ceases to be a cube of ice, it ceases to be. Science teaches that when a cube of ice ceases to be a cube of ice, it does *not* cease to be: for a cube of ice is really just a sample of H_2O that happens to be in a low-energy state, in which the molecules are arranged in a lattice.

But my point is not just that science *does* say that when the cubes on my counter have melted, nothing really has been destroyed, but that this is an *empirically approvable* thing to say. This interpretation of the data enables predictions and explanations not available if I merely supposed that ice cubes had been destroyed, to be replaced by something different. It enables me to explain why the liquid that remains is clear and odorless. It enables me to predict that, and understand why, the liquid will turn to vapor if I continue to leave the dish out on the counter; also that, and why, ice can be formed again out of the liquid that has now supplanted the cubes; even that, and why, both processes will happen at particular rates given particular temperatures.

3.1   Apparent Destruction as Really Just Alteration: An Empirically Defensible Claim?

But what really is so bad, my opponent might ask—what really is so different from the ice-and-water case—about the general idea that where a packet of properties vanishes, which both my test and common sense think of as composing the essential nature of some natural kind, all that really has happened is some alteration? Let me begin on the argument by considering a version of this general view that *everyone* would agree to be empirically worthless and empty.

Observe Max, sprinting down the sidewalk to catch a bus that is just now starting to shut its doors. Max should have been more careful about the time. The afternoon is oppressively humid, and a light rain has started to fall; Max should be avoiding such strenuous exertion since he is fighting a cold, and should probably have taken the time to put on the light raincoat that is now stuffed into his bag. But suddenly a bolt of lightning splits the sky. Suddenly it turns out that there is a different and worse reason why Max would have been better off to have gotten to the bus stop earlier. Max is struck by the lightning and killed instantly. I omit details, but Max is partly vaporized.

Common sense supposes that exactly when and where Max is struck by lightning, an existence ends. It is plausible to suppose that the test of flanking uniformities would support the same judgment. In 7.4 I will set forth reasons for supposing that human beings compose unto themselves a distinct natural kind. Just which properties are those that essentially characterize members of this kind is ultimately a question for empirical research, just as is the question of what the essential properties of human brains are. But it seems certain that whatever these properties turn out to be,

when the test of flanking uniformities is applied to the
empirical data, many of them will have just now ceased to
obtain, where Max was struck by the lightning. The test of
flanking uniformities will corroborate the judgment of
common sense.

But suppose someone were to claim—for the sake of
argument, I will volunteer the claim myself—that nothing
has actually been destroyed in the case described. All that
really has happened is that something has undergone an
alteration. Suppose specifically I claimed that all that has
happened is that my *desk* has undergone an alteration,
even though miles removed from the scene involving Max.
What common sense thinks of as the destruction of Max, I
would claim, is just a matter of my desk's passing from one
phase to another—from coexisting with Max to coexisting
with mere scraps of Max's body. Certainly *this* interpretation of the data about Max *would* be empirically empty, and
far different from the claim that all that really happened in
the dish on my counter was that a certain volume of H_2O
had passed from one molecular arrangement to another.
But why, exactly? The latter claim explained features of
the liquid that remained after the alteration, and predicted
things that might in the future be expected to happen to that
liquid. Why does it explain nothing about my desk's current
state, nor predict anything about its possible future states,
to view my desk as undergoing the "alteration" in question?
For that matter, why does the "alteration" in question
neither predict nor explain what things will for a time
be like, at the particular place where Max was struck by
lightning?

The rough intuitive answer is that neither the *before*
phase nor the *after* phase in this so-called alteration are
genuine phases in my desk's own course of existence. There

are two ways to put this more crisply. One is to say that neither the *before* phase nor the *after* phase figure in the causal chains which link earlier episodes to later ones in the existence of my desk. Neither phase reflects my desk's past nor has bearing on how, in actual and possible subsequent episodes, my desk will look or act. In contrast, the *before* phase in the alteration on my kitchen counter reflects the cubes' having been in the freezer, and the *after* phase bears on possible evaporation or refreezing.

The other way of sharpening the same basic idea is to say that the alteration that my desk allegedly underwent involves ineliminably the existence, in addition to the desk, of Max himself. There seems to be no way of conceptualizing either the *before* or the *after* as a phase involving *merely* the desk—involving its intrinsic properties, its dispositions, the relations to its surroundings that influence or could influence its properties, and so on.

The shade of difference between these two sharpenings is worth preserving. I suggest we consider there to be *two* general requirements on any position claiming that when a familiar object appears to have been destroyed, what really has happened is just that something has been altered. First, the alteration in question must grow out of, and have bearing on, the course of existence of that "something." Second, it must be possible to conceptualize the alteration as involving *only* the existence and circumstances of that "something": we must not be required to quantify over the familiar object that common sense supposes to have been destroyed, on pain of admitting that there is *both* an alteration *and* a destruction.

Thus the empirical defensibility of the "alteration only" view depends on just *what* is said to have altered, where common sense and my test alike espy a destruction. In the rest of this chapter I will examine variations of the answer that what has altered is the *matter* of which the familiar object (e.g., Max) is composed. But there is an answer to which I shall not be giving serious consideration. This is the view that where common sense and my test espy the destruction of a person—or of a quartz crystal or an atom of gold or a tree—all that really has happened is that precisely *that* object has undergone an alteration. There is such a view. It is called by Alan Sidelle "bizarre reductionism" (Sidelle 1998, pp. 432–436). It claims not to deny that there are in the world familiar objects such as people and trees, but only to attribute to such objects unsuspected capacities for survival. People continue to exist even when vaporized by lightning, on this view, and a tree survives passage through a wood chipper. Given favorable tradewinds, then, a person can fly across the ocean without the benefit of an airplane. Trees can be strewn on the floor of a restaurant to create "atmosphere," and small children can pick up handfuls of trees and toss them into the air. I suppose Sidelle is right to call this view "bizarre." In any case it seems to me too contrived to be worthy of discussion. I shall construe the "alteration only" view as asserting, not that familiar objects such as trees and humans survive where common sense supposes them to be destroyed, but that there simply are no such objects in the first place. Instead there are various units of matter, units that during certain phases wear all the properties characteristic of such familiar objects, but which continue to exist upon dropping such properties.

3.2   Physical Simples Arranged Human-wise

Let me begin with the version of the "alteration only" view that seems most likely to withstand my objection. My objection says that the data that the test of flanking uniformities interprets as the destruction of a familiar object—namely, the disappearance of a package of "essential" properties—cannot with equal empirical warrant be interpreted as a mere alteration in some matter. The version most likely to withstand this objection, it would seem, is the one that offers the most scientifically grounded picture of the matter in question. Consider then the subatomic microparticles that future physics will discover to be the truly fundamental building blocks of the physical world—"physical simples," as they often are called. The first version of the "alteration only" view says this: where it seems that a familiar object such as Max has been destroyed, all that really has happened is that physical simples formerly arranged in a certain way, for example physical simples human-wise arranged, have come to be arranged differently.[1]

Of course one might ask: just *which* physical simples come to be differently arranged, when common sense supposes Max to have been destroyed; *which* physical simples formerly were, and no longer are, human-wise arranged? There is after all "the problem of the many" (Unger 1980; cf. van Inwagen 1990, p. 214ff.). This is the problem that if one tries to specify the boundaries of a familiar medium-sized object at the level of individual microparticles, one finds that (vastly) many incompatible specifications are equally warranted. But it would be captious for us to dwell on this challenge. The apparent destruction of a familiar object embroils not just the microparticles on its disputed boundaries, but also all that definitely lie within those boundaries. My opponent can say that at least the latter microparticles have passed from being human-wise arranged to being otherwise arranged, and that that is what the "destruction" of Max really amounts to.

The far harder question for my opponent is *what it is* for a particular plurality of microparticles to be "human-wise arranged." The too-easy answer is that this is for each of the microparticles to be contained within (perhaps *definitely* within) the boundaries of one and the same human. This is too easy since if there are in the world no such familiar objects as humans, there is in the world no such property as *being contained within the boundaries of a human*. And the proponent of "alteration only" must, to repeat, say that there are in the world no such objects as humans; otherwise he is just saying that the destruction of Max, which common sense and my test alike recognize, is *accompanied by* an alteration in Max's matter, rather than that it is in serious ontology *replaced by* an alteration in that matter.

It is also too easy an answer to say that for microparticles to be "human-wise arranged" is for them to lie within a spatial region in which we humans *imagine* there to be a single human. (This is the "fictionalist" answer discussed but not endorsed in Merricks 2001, pp. 3–8.) The problem here is not so much that the analysans affirms after all the existence of humans, as agents of the imagining in question. The real problem is wholly general, and concerns what my opponent puts in place of the apparent destruction of *any* familiar object, whether a human or a tree (alteration from "tree-wise arranged" to otherwise) or a quartz crystal (first "quartz-crystal-wise arranged," then not), and so on. The real problem is that my opponent has promised to tell us of an alteration which really is going on, in ontological strictness, where common sense merely imagines the destruction of a familiar object. This real alteration cannot just *consist in* common sense's imagining what it does. It must have a real *before* phase and a real *after* phase and the two phases must really be distinct. But there is no real distinction between certain microparticles' lying within the imaginary borders of imaginary objects, and their lying no longer within those imaginary borders.

Or might my opponent argue that though microparticles' being arranged human-wise cannot *consist in* their imaginary occupancy of imaginary borders, it may lie in what *causes* our imaginings that a human is present here and there and there? Perhaps our employment of our concept of a human, in occasion-judgments that a human is now before us, causally reflects exactly those microphysical properties and relations among microparticles in which "human-wise arrangement" consists. And perhaps our occasion-indexed employments of our concepts of a tree or of a statue likewise reveal what it is for microparticles to be tree-wise and statue-wise arranged. This is the sort of answer on tree-wise and statue-wise arrangement that Merricks endorses. "What the folk mean by 'statue,'" he writes, "is part of what makes it the case that certain atomic features are those upon which, if there were statues, statue composition would supervene" (2001, p. 7).

But note that if my opponent elects this sort of answer on what it is for microparticles to be statue-wise arranged—and, by extension, on what it is for microparticles to be human-wise arranged—he commits himself to an answer that is not too easy, but on the contrary very hard indeed to spell out. There are many real episodes of causing, we must now suppose, in which *these* (many) microparticles and *those* (many) microparticles and *those* (many) microparticles all participate, all of which result in a tokening by us folk of the folk concept of a human. In virtue of which properties and relations are the microparticles involved in each of these causings the ones that *are* involved—in virtue of what is it *not* the case that *more* microparticles or *fewer* are involved?

What ties each plurality of microparticles together, at the microphysical level, and what is common or recurrent in the ways each plurality is tied together?

I presently will argue that it is unwarranted to suppose that these questions have answers at all. But I agree with Merricks that the general sort of analysis of "human-wise arranged" or "tree-wise arranged" that my opponent must give, in order to argue that the apparent destruction of a human or a tree is really just the alteration of certain microparticles from human-wise or tree-wise arrangement to different arrangements, has exactly this shape. Nothing so easy as containment within a human's borders, or containment in a region where a human is imagined to be, can be my opponent's answer to what it is for microparticles to be "human-wise arranged." The real answer must point not to a relation that each microparticle in a plurality so arranged bears to a common familiar object, but rather to a relation (or a system of relations) that each microparticle in such a plurality bears to others in the plurality—ultimately, to a relation that each bears to *all* the others and *only* the others in the plurality. Or if there is ineliminable vagueness about just which microparticles are at any one time and place "human-wise arranged," the relation must tie each to all those others that definitely *are* "human-wise arranged" along with the given microparticle, and to none that definitely is *not*, and must neither quite *tie* each nor quite *not tie* each to all microparticles in the vague border.

Just what relation (or system of relations) might my opponent cite? First let us remind ourselves just which microparticles we expect to see brought together in this relation's grasp. Return then to Max, running to catch the bus. Despite the hair gel Max uses, his hair is flying in the wind; also, his glasses are starting to slip off the bridge of his nose; and his shirttail is flapping behind him. Meanwhile there is the cold that Max is fighting: rhinovirus organisms are present in many of his alveoli.

Just which relation joins each microparticle within Max to all others within him, and to none that composes Max's clothes and coverings, nor the invaders in Max's body? One answer that can quickly be dismissed is the relation of "fellow-traveling"—the relation that obtains between microparticle a and microparticle b just in case there is a reliable connection between a's moving rapidly south or north along the sidewalk and b's moving rapidly south or north along the sidewalk (compare proposition [A], van Inwagen 1990, p. 105). For the microparticles in Max's hair gel "fellow travel" with those in Max's heart, every bit as much as do the microparticles in Max's scalp; so too do the microparticles in Max's shirttail, in the molecules of air trapped within the shirttail, and in the rhinoviruses in Max's lungs. At the same time at least some microparticles in Max's facial epidermis fail to "fellow travel" with these others: they are abraded by the wind as Max runs.

What my opponent needs to identify, surely, is a relation that is not merely spatial but causal. We need not pause to debate whether ". . . is a cause of . . ." is transitive, though in chapter 4 I shall argue that it is not. For even if it is nontransitive, we can define an ancestral of it such that if an alteration in microparticle a causes an alteration in microparticle b, and an alteration in microparticle b causes an alteration in microparticle c, the alteration in microparticle a bears this ancestral causal relation to the alteration in microparticle c. "Exerts some measure of causal influence over" might be a good name for such a long-reaching relation.

But it seems hard to believe that events befalling an individual microparticle within, say, one of Max's hairs do exert some causal influence over what happens to some individual microparticle in Max's kneecap, while events befalling an individual microparticle in Max's hair *gel* do *not*. It is even hard to believe that there is some one *degree* of causal influence such that the state of an individual microparticle in an individual hair exerts influence of that degree or greater, on the state of an individual kneecap microparticle, but an individual microparticle in Max's hair gel exerts an influence of only a lesser degree. It seems, rather, that an individual microparticle within, say, Max's heart exerts about as much causal influence over what happens to an individual microparticle in the bows of Max's glasses, as over what happens to any individual microparticle in Max's eyelids. For the laws of microphysics that underwrite such causal influence take no account of whether an individual microparticle being causally influenced, or an individual microparticle exercising such causal influence, are located in a plastic object or in an organic one.

Now I do admit that *this* seems plausible: that if *all* the microparticles composing Max's heart were suddenly to undergo some cataclysmic alteration, this *would* soon make some large difference in the careers of the microparticles composing Max's eyelids, a difference greater than any difference made in the careers of the microparticles composing Max's glasses. But can my opponent at this point trade on this thought? The view he is trying to articulate is that familiar objects—including even hearts and eyelids—do not really ever get destroyed, and do not indeed exist. Instead certain pluralities of microparticles pass from being heart-wise or lung-wise or eyelid-wise arranged to being differently arranged. But these pluralities have determinate, if imprecise, membership; and my opponent's task at present is to say what it is for just *those* microparticles, not more or fewer, to make up such a plurality, and to say this in a way that does not quantify over familiar objects. So the challenge that my opponent faces in regard to Max himself is a challenge that he also faces in regard to Max's heart and eyelids and glasses. He needs to *earn* the right to speak of "all the microparticles composing Max's heart."

The way for him to earn such a right is, we have seen, for him to identify causal relations that tie individual microparticles within that object to all and only the rest. But the prospects for doing this are poor. An individual *cell* in Max's eyelids can undergo a rich variety of changes, both healthy and unhealthy, and this is a large part of the reason why Max's heart can exercise great causal influence over the state of such a cell—far greater influence than it exercises over the state of Max's glasses. But an individual *microparticle* in Max's eyelids can undergo only a narrowly defined range of state changes and motions. Hence there are only a *few* ways in which an individual *microparticle in* Max's heart can influence the state of an individual microparticle in Max's eyelids; it can only, in an extremely indirect and mediated way, influence motions or state changes in that individual microparticle. But it can also, in an equally indirect and mediated way, influence motions and state changes in an individual microparticle just beyond (what common sense sees as) the surface of Max's skin, or even well beyond it; and an individual microparticle outside Max's body altogether—say, in the air blowing on Max's eyelid—can likewise influence the individual microparticles in Max's eyelids.

I now lay my cards on the table: no causal relation holds each of the microparticles within a familiar medium-sized object together with all and only the others—not even *roughly* all and *roughly* only the others. So my opponent cannot say what "being human-wise arranged" amounts to without quantifying over humans (or what "being glasses-wise arranged" amounts to without quantifying over eye-glasses, etc.). He cannot defend the claim that there even *is* such a state of affairs, obtaining among microparticles, unless he affirms that there are in the world humans.

3.3   An Objection Dismissed

But there is one sort of case—exceptional but not unthink-able—which may make the position I have just laid on the table seem exaggerated. Suppose that Max stares so intently at the bus he is chasing that he runs full-speed into a waist-high post. Or suppose, less unpleasantly, that a billiard ball is struck sharply by a cue stick. In either case microparticles at the point of impact undergo very sharp alterations in their energy states. They then exercise considerable causal influence over neighboring microparticles, altering their energy states in turn. Thus are causal chains launched that at length embroil, let us suppose, every last microparticle within Max or the billiard ball. Finally let us suppose that these chains at length *converge* on a single microparticle within Max or within the ball. Then that one microparticle has been causally influenced, to a high degree, by all and only the other microparticles in the familiar object that common sense recognizes. The microparticle membership of that familiar object has been recaptured at the level of a causal relation between microparticles.

But note two things about such an example. First, only one microparticle within the familiar object is causally influenced by every last other microparticle within it, and by only those others. The vast majority of microparticles in the familiar object, even on the fanciful hypothesis of convergence, are causally influenced by (and themselves in turn causally influence) only *some* other microparticles within the object. Those at the point of impact moreover are highly influenced by microparticles *not* within the object. Second, the one microparticle that does momentarily stand in a relation reflecting the exact microparticle composition of the familiar object does so only now, only once. It is *too* fanciful to suppose that on other occasions of impact, that very microparticle will again be *the* one on which all causal chains converge.

What far, far more commonly happens is that relations of causal influence link an individual microparticle within a familiar object now to some others within the object, now to different others within it, now to microparticles largely outside the object. There is no causal relation that, as a general matter, joins individual microparticles within a given familiar object to all and only the others that are within it. *At the level of microphysics, the microparticle membership of a familiar medium-sized object is causally invisible.*

But if so, the claim I made earlier involves no exaggeration after all. There is simply no way for the champion of "alteration only" to defend the idea that there is in the world such a phenomenon as microparticles' being "human-wise arranged," unless he concedes that there are in the world humans. So he cannot contend that the apparent destruction of a human is supplanted, in strict ontology, by a mere alteration—one that begins with just that phenomenon, and ends with the microparticles being otherwise arranged.

3.4   Alteration in Aggregates and in Lumps

Or might my opponent argue that the alteration that replaces, in serious ontology, the apparent destruction of a familiar object is an alteration involving not many objects but one—not, for example, the microparticles arranged human-wise where Max seems to be, but the collection of microparticles that composes Max? If my opponent can make out that there is such a collection, he surely can claim that it undergoes a very real (and very violent) alteration when Max is struck by lightning. Both the *before* phase and the *after* phase of that alteration seem truly to be phases proper to that collection's own course of existence. The *before* phase will have grown smoothly out of that collection's past, and the *after* phase will have left an indelible imprint on that collection's future.

In this section I argue that my opponent cannot have it both ways. He can argue that there really is such a collection of microparticles, in a world from which Max himself is strictly absent, but cannot then point to a way the alteration shapes that collection's course of existence. Or he can point to a collection whose career *is* greatly influenced by the fateful bolt of lightning, but it will be a collection whose reality is covertly parasitic on the reality of Max.

For the phrase "the collection of microparticles that composes Max" can be read in different ways. Let us first take it to mean the *aggregate* of microparticles, found exactly where Max is found (and let us set aside, for the moment, the worry that Max's borders are not exact). An *aggregate* of microparticles is the mereological sum of individually specified microparticles. It continues to exist as long as just *those* individual microparticles all continue to exist, and just where those individual microparticles exist.

Now Max, like any familiar medium-sized object, is (in Dean Zimmerman's phrase) mereologically incontinent (*if* Max exists at all). Individual microparticles are constantly departing from Max's body; also, others are constantly entering it. Some of these entering microparticles may intu-itively seem to be invaders, but others seem intuitively to be taken up into Max's body, to enter into its composition—for example, all those that get lodged in Max's bloodstream. So over the course of Max's brief life, he is composed of a whole series of distinct aggregates of microparticles. Just which aggregate should my opponent pick, as the one whose alteration is all that the apparent destruction of Max really amounts to? For now, I will suppose that my opponent answers: the aggregate of microparticles found within Max's borders at the very moment before the bolt of light-ning strikes.

Can it really be said that the bolt of lightning interrupts or disrupts the previous career of this aggregate of micro-particles? Or that it exercises profound influence over this aggregate's future career? My opponent presumably says both: his claim is presumably that the lightning strike amounts to a violent change of course in the career of this aggregate. But does this aggregate really even *have* a career long enough to enable my opponent to discern within it both a previous phase and a subsequent phase?

If this aggregate of microparticles does have a temporally protracted career, that career seems in any case not to have begun in advance of Max's own existence. I am not denying that that aggregate *existed* before Max was born or con-ceived; it surely did exist. But it was, for vast periods before Max's birth, strikingly scattered in space. Over these vast periods it was *too* scattered, it seems, to have as a whole caused anything, or to have undergone any unitary reac-tions to impinging events. Microphysics would have had no greater need to recognize its existence, during these vast periods, than the existence of any other gerrymandered or randomly assembled collection of microparticles. All that this aggregate *did*, during these vast stretches of its existence, was to *be* the collection that it is.

Yet during at least a short time leading up to Max's death, my opponent might rejoin, that very aggregate *can* be said to have done many things—to have produced many effects. For Max himself did many things during just this short time. He talked on the phone to a friend, let us say, and posted a payment on his phone bill. Every action Max took, my opponent might plausibly claim, supervened on complex microphysical events involving the microparticles that composed him (perhaps together with complex microphysical events involving microparticles that surrounded Max). So the microparticles that composed Max, at the moments of the morning of his death, themselves produced many effects. Now it is true—this my opponent would have to allow— that not *every* one of the microparticles in the aggregate affected by the lightning strike was present *in* Max during all these moments. Max took a breath of air just seconds before the lightning strike, and the microparticles in those oxygen atoms, taken up into Max's bloodstream by the precise moment of the strike, were not present in Max's body during any of Max's activities that morning. Even so, a vast majority of the microparticles comprised in the ill-fated aggregate *were* present in Max throughout the morning. This vast majority jointly produced many complex microphysical events over the course of the morning. So surely, my opponent might insist, that aggregate itself might be said to have done much over the course of the morning. Its career can be said to extend at least that far back.

But I question whether this really *can* be said. Certainly it does not *follow*, from the premise that a part of x caused effect e, that x caused effect e, even if the part is large—that reasoning embodies the fallacy of composition. In a case like the present one, such a conclusion appears to be not just unwarranted but extremely implausible. The precise reason why it is implausible depends on the precise analysis of causation one elects; the conclusion is implausible on any analysis currently on offer, but for different reasons in different cases. I will limit myself to saying why it is implausible on the analysis I will endorse and articulate in chapter 4. That analysis comes from Mackie by way of Bennett, and says that for event c to be a cause of event e is for c to be an *NS* condition of e (Bennett 1988, ch. 3). That is, it is for c to be a Necessary component of circumstances and developments that actually preceded e and which jointly were Sufficient for e. Suppose then that forty minutes before his death, Max wrote a check to the phone company. The appearance of letters and numbers on the check, my opponent supposes, supervened on a complex microphysical outcome caused by a complex set of motions and state changes involving the microparticles that composed Max's body. Is this enough to establish that the aggregate a of microparticles, composing Max *at the time of the lightning strike*, itself caused the appearance of the letters and numbers—or at least caused the complex microphysical outcome e on which that appearance supervened? For this to be true, on the Mackie–Bennett understanding of causation, some state of affairs involving a itself—*including* the microparticles in the oxygen Max breathed in just a second before his death—would have had to figure indispensably in the circumstances that obtained and were jointly sufficient for e. But this is extremely implausible. Surely even if those individual oxygen atoms breathed in by Max in his last breath had not even *been in existence* forty minutes before his death—even if there had not then *existed* aggregate a—outcome e would have occurred anyway, and Max would have written the check. *Nothing* involving *a* was indispensable to *that* outcome.

I conclude that the aggregate of microparticles composing Max at the moment of the lightning strike had a career that had begun at most one second before. After the lightning strike, that aggregate was again too scattered to be said to have *done* anything as a unitary whole, or to have been influenced as a unitary whole. Indeed the career of this aggregate would seem to have extended over just a single episode: all it did was to get violently scattered. Its "getting scattered" did not interrupt or break the pattern of an earlier career, and did not leave an indelible imprint on a later career. That episode did not comprise a *before* phase that grew smoothly out of a past history of that aggregate and an *after* phase reflected in that aggregate's subsequent history. The "getting scattered" was the *whole* history of the aggregate: the getting scattered cannot be seen as an *alteration* proper to that aggregate's *course* of existence.

(To be candid, I think it is questionable whether there even *is* such an entity as the aggregate of microparticles that composes Max at the moment of his death. The main reason for thinking so is the doctrine of unrestricted mereological composition, a.k.a. universalism. But from the standpoint of my starting assumption—that ontology should operate under empirical load, giving preference to just those objects that our folk or learned theories about the world find it useful to posit—that doctrine appears suspect. The burden of proof is on its proponents [see the introduction] and not, as is sometimes supposed,[2] on its opponents. That aside, there are arguments against it. In chapter 7 I argue that mereological sums of microparticles—and the argument generalizes—would, if real, have essential properties that do not test *as* essential on any realist test. In chapter 4 I argue that true laws of nature do not apply to randomly assembled aggregates of microparticles. Thus if any true causing must be subsumed under some law of nature, such aggregates cause nothing, which for many will impugn their reality. These objections seem to me to overwhelm the only real *argument* in favor of universalism that I know of, namely Sider's [1997, pp. 216–222]. That argument relies on the assumption that there must in any finite world be a precise whole number of "concrete objects" [p. 221]. But what is it for an object to be "concrete"? If Sider had some positive answer, he could argue that there cannot, in the nature of the case, be borderline instances of such objects—cases, for example, in which it is indeterminate whether concrete object *b* is a distinct object from concrete object *a*. But Sider's only characterization [p. 221] is privative and open-ended: to be concrete is to be not a set and not a property and not a universal and not. . . .)

But now let the champion of "alteration only" return to the starting point of this section, and read "the collection of microparticles composing Max" differently. Collections of microparticles do not *have* to be construed as aggregates, after all. We can instead think of a "collection of microparticles" as comprising different members at different times. We can suppose that, as individual microparticles get stripped from Max's epidermis by the abrasion of the wind, and as new microparticles get added to Max by his breathing in of oxygen, "the collection of microparticles which composes Max" loses some members and adds others—it alters in membership, but continues to exist. In short we may individuate "collections of microparticles" in the same way some philosophers—for example, Alan Sidelle—individuate "lumps of matter" (Sidelle 1998, pp. 426–430). A given lump can survive departure or destruction of some component bits, but not of all, and just *how many* departures it can survive (or how many additions sustain) will be a matter fixed by context or by stipulation.

So conceived, the collection of microparticles that composes Max at the time of the lightning strike can claim a career that reaches fairly far back in time: it is the same collection as composed Max when he wrote the check. Thus here we *do* have a subject of alteration that has a whole *course* of existence, a course altered and reshaped (or deshaped) by the lightning strike. But can alteration in *this* collection of microparticles satisfy the other requirement (3.1) on an alteration that supplants, in serious ontology, the apparent destruction of a familiar object—can we specify what the alteration involves, and what undergoes it, without quantifying over Max himself?

The collection of microparticles that composes Max, my opponent will say, occupies exactly the same space as Max does, at all moments in its career up until Max's death. But *in virtue of what* does it do this: what *about* that collection makes it false to say that, at some of these moments, it is located elsewhere? My opponent cannot answer that it is after all just *that* collection of microparticles (just *that* lump of matter) which, during Max's existence, composes Max. For Max himself does not strictly exist, on my opponent's official view, whereas this collection of microparticles does. So my opponent must rather say that the path apparently taken by Max, at various points in his apparent existence, merely marks out for common sense the regions occupied by this collection, and is not *constitutive of* this occupancy. But then what *is* constitutive of this collection's occupying, at any given moment, the full volume that it does? My opponent must identify a relation (or system of relations) that binds together all the individual microparticles within the collection, and captures no microparticles outside it—and the relation must be a real microphysical relation that the microparticles bear to all and only one another, not an imaginary relation that they bear to the imaginary Max. Yet there is no such microphysical relation (or system of relations), as we noted in the previous section.

I should add a word on a certain variant of the kind of "collection of microparticles" that has an extended career and is shifting in its membership. The membership conditions for such a collection, we have noted, are looser than those for membership in an aggregate. To some philosophers the looseness of the conditions will suggest vagueness in composition, and vagueness in composition will seem to be trouble (though see chapter 6). Hence some philosophers will prefer to think of what alters, when it appears to common sense that Max is destroyed, as a four-dimensional object. Its temporal parts are precisely defined aggregates, each found where some appropriate precisification of Max (were he but real) exists (cf. Sider 1997, pp. 223 ff.). Against this four-dimensional object I lodge the same objection *mutatis mutandis* as against the three-dimensional enduring collection (or lump) that it replaces. Why are just *these* moment-long aggregates the ones bound together in the career of a temporally extended object—why not, at each moment, an aggregate comprising more microparticles or fewer? What binds together the microparticles in each time-slice cannot be their relation to *Max*. But neither can it be microphysical relations that they bear to all and only one another.

3.5   Alterations in Prime Matter

But microparticles and collections of microparticles might not be the best vehicles for articulating the thought that when a familiar object appears to have been destroyed, what really has happened is that something else has altered. What about the case in which a fundamental microparticle itself appears to have been destroyed? At one moment the properties distinctive of, say, a top quark are present at a particular location, and at the very next the properties of a bottom quark are there instead. Consistency seems to require that the basic thought be expanded: even when it appears that a *microparticle* has been destroyed, what really has happened is that some yet more fundamental stuff or object has taken on a different form (cf. Sidelle 1998, pp. 438–440). Microphysics may indeed determine that the case envisioned is fanciful—that it simply cannot happen, as a matter of physical law, that any fundamental microparticle *either* just vanishes *or* turns into a microparticle of a different kind. But there would still be possible worlds in which the actual laws of physics do not hold—or so many of my opponents suppose, though in 2.6 I gave my own reasons for disagreeing—and in many of them, my opponents will say, the case envisioned will really occur. Consistency does seem to require us to say that in such a case a parcel of more fundamental stuff merely alters—that it loses the top quark form and acquires the bottom quark form, while continuing to exist—and if so, we seemingly must say that in the actual world too, microparticles are just specifically formed parcels of the more fundamental stuff.

What nature should we think of this more fundamental stuff as having? An ancient and recurrent thought has been that we only postpone our problems, and do not solve them, if we think of this stuff as having, intrinsically, any constitutive nature at all. For if we think of it as having any constitutive nature, we will have to face cases in which a chunk of it is apparently destroyed. It will be of no more avail here than it was before to say that such cases are nomologically impossible. What we really must conceive of, then, is a sub-strate of change concerning which it is *logically* impossible, not just *nomologically* impossible, that it should lose its con-stitutive nature and thus cease to exist. This can only be a stuff that *has*, intrinsically, no constitutive nature. It will be such as to acquire a nature—an accidental nature—only when and to the extent that it comes to be formed in this way or that.

Such essenceless "stuff" (or "world-stuff") has been posited by Alan Sidelle (1989), as we have seen (1.2)—though sometimes rather guardedly (Sidelle 1998)—and likewise by Michael Jubien (1993). Michael Dummett in passing expresses support for the concept (1973, p. 577). Kant squarely supports it in many passages in the First Analogy (and appears to retract his support in other pas-sages).[3] But I shall call it "prime matter," since that is what traditional commentary on Aristotle (1966) calls it—though, to be fair, Aristotle himself seems more nearly to be cornered into affirming its existence, than to do so willingly.[4]

When the lightning appeared to destroy Max, then, what really happened is that a large amount of prime matter acquired a different form. But did that event constitute an alteration proper to that prime matter's career, its own course of existence? Did that re-forming figure squarely in the causal chains which tied earlier episodes to later ones in that prime matter's existence?

A preliminary question: *are there* any such causal chains? If there are, they evidently cannot take the form that is famil-iar to everyday thought. Later stages in the career of a dog or a sweater or a building are shaped by earlier ones in ways *reflective of the kind* to which these items belong: a sweater responds differently to application of hot water, or to being folded, from how a building does, and both respond differently to angry shouts from how a dog does. But later states in the "life" of a particular amount or parcel of prime matter cannot, it seems, grow out of earlier stages in ways *reflective of its nature*, of the kind to which it belongs. For prime matter *has* after all no constitutive nature.

Or might something *like* a nature get fashioned, for a particular parcel or amount of prime matter, out of the accidents of its history? Might it simply be a law of nature that prime matter that once held the form of a human were afterwards equipped with certain capacities for becoming differently formed, and specific incapacities for acquiring yet other forms? In that case the alteration that the prime matter composing Max underwent, at the time of the lightning strike, might indeed amount to an alteration proper to its own existence. The *after* phase of this alteration would have opened that prime matter toward a future in which it could take on new forms, but the *before* phase would have limited the forms it could take on to a specified range; the prime matter would have been channeled, say, toward a future in which it might acquire the form of a butterfly or a daisy, but could not acquire the form of paving material.

But how firmly would the alteration have channeled this prime matter's future development; how deep would be the impress of this prime matter's past as a human? One possible answer would be that the impress of the past could simply wear off. Prime matter once formed as a human, for example, could after a time simply drop its incapacity to become paving material, and could after all take on just that form. But this answer would make it unclear how that same prime matter's future as a butterfly might truly reflect its humaniform past: the distinction between reflecting this past and violating this past seems lost. Hence the proponent of prime matter might well prefer the alternative answer:

the impress of the past is deep. Prime matter that once acquires the accident of being formed as a human is, by virtue of the laws of nature, stamped ever thereafter with specific incapacities and specific dispositions.

Yet now the proponent of prime matter himself faces a question much like that raised against the champion of microparticles. That question was, what if at one instant a microparticle is present at a given location bearing the properties characteristic of a top quark, and at the next instant, a microparticle bearing the properties characteristic of a bottom quark? True, this question apparently asks about a world in which the actual laws of nature do not hold. Even so, it seemed that the champion of microparticles had to give some answer. So too, here, must the proponent of prime matter. What if at one moment prime matter with the specific capacities characteristic of ex-human prime matter were present at a given location, and at the very next moment prime matter with different capacities were present at that very location—with the capacities of, say, ex-building prime matter? Should we say that the original prime matter had been destroyed, and replaced with a different parcel of prime matter? Or does consistency with the top quark case require the proponent of prime matter to posit *alteration* here, rather than destruction? Should he say that what was *formed as* prime matter with the fixed capacities of ex-human prime matter has come to be *formed as* prime matter with different fixed capacities? Should he, that is, posit a kind of Ur–prime matter, which can get formed as prime matter with one set of capacities *or* as prime matter with a different set?

It would be a mistake to give either answer. It is only through confusion that the choice between them even arises. For prime matter was at the outset conceived as a sort of stuff for which even the suspicion of destruction could not logically arise—a stuff that is proof against destruction, not just nomologically, but logically. So rather than answer the question "What if it appears that a parcel of prime matter has been destroyed?," the proponent of prime matter should reject its premise. Prime matter, he must say, does not come with different fixed features. Whatever the forms it has assumed in the past, all prime matter is alike.

But then the prime matter that composes the fragments and shards of Max is effectively unmarked by its past. Whatever the forms we imagine this prime matter assuming in the future, there is no question of its assumption of them violating its past. Nor is there any question of its assumption of them *reflecting* its past: whatever the forms this prime matter does subsequently assume, *that* it assumes them in no way reflects its past as a human. *There are* no causal links by which the past of this prime matter shapes its present, or its present constrains its future. So the alteration this prime matter undergoes during the explosion does not figure in such links.

The change, then, from *composing-a-human* to *no-longer-composing-a-human* is not a change proper to the career, the course of existence, of the prime matter that composed Max. It is a mere "Cambridge change." *Any* change that happens to prime matter is a "Cambridge change"—that is the cost of being unmarked by the past, and featureless in essential nature. It is pointless, then, to maintain that the apparent destruction of any familiar object is really just an alteration in the career of some prime matter. For the "alteration" in question is always just as empty as the "alteration" undergone by my desk, when Max was struck by lightning.

II

Causal Exclusion and
Compositional
Vagueness

4   Mental Causation versus Physical Causation: Coincidences and Accidents

Are there objects in the world that trace out mind-independent courses of existence? Part I has shown how we can give a positive answer to this question. It is fairly evident *that* we must give a positive answer, chapter 1 argued; the thesis that there are no objects having mind-independent existence is self-defeating. But it is far less evident *how* to give a positive answer. For doing so requires viewing the essentialness of the properties essential to the world's objects—of the properties they must cling to over their courses of existence—as a status those properties enjoy mind-independently. Yet there is a long-standing puzzle as to how, if essentialness is mind-independent, we could ever detect it. And detect it we surely do. But chapter 2 argued that the puzzle is the product of a lack of self-awareness. In fact we do wield a philosophically defensible test for essentialness, and that test is wholly empirical, thus permitting us to view essentialness as something independent, not mind-bestowed, after all. It is mistaken to worry that this test (the "test of flanking uniformities") tests not for whether a property is essential to the objects that bear it, but only for whether it is a necessary condition for those objects to belong to one or another natural kind. That worry rests on the idea that the objects that populate the world can lose membership in a given natural kind without ceasing to exist. But chapter 3 showed we must suppose the world to contain objects for which kind-membership is a life-and-death issue, even if it also is true that there is the matter of which they are composed, and that this matter survives the destruction of such objects.

But *how many* objects, among those that scientifically informed common sense appears to believe in, can be said to trace out mind-independent existences? Many philosophers believe or worry that there are deep reasons for doubting that familiar medium-sized objects are among those that can be said, in ontological strictness, to exist. In the present part, I confront two such reasons. The first is furnished by "causal exclusion" arguments—arguments that the causation apparently exercised by familiar objects is everywhere shadowed by causation exercised by the microparticles of physics. Unless we can believe there is ubiquitous overdetermination, the two levels of causation appear to be in competition, and the causation at the microparticle level seems to have the stronger claim to being genuine. But this leaves familiar objects in apparent violation of Alexander's dictum that "to be real is to have causal powers." The most familiar causal exclusion arguments are those focused on mental causation, and I consider them in this present chapter. Is the causation apparently exercised by people as thinking agents—by people in virtue of their having the beliefs and desires they do—preempted by causation exercised by the microparticles within them, or elsewhere located? In this chapter I argue that the answer is No: the outcomes that people as agents produce cannot be seen as the work of microparticles. But causal exclusion arguments also seem to apply, as often is recognized,[1] to causation apparently exercised not just by minds but by the large-sized agents recognized by any of the special sciences—for example, by evolutionary biology or economics. In chapter 5 I argue that the causal efficacy of these large objects is not preempted by the actions of microparticles, since what those large objects bring about could not be effected except by microparticles too scattered and disconnected to be able to cause anything.

The other reason for worry that familiar medium-sized objects may not really exist in the world has to do with vagueness. Many of the properties characteristic of such objects appear to be vague—sorites arguments seem to show that if such properties are present in clear-cut cases, they must also be present in cases where no one can believe them to be present. For philosophers comfortable with the idea that familiar objects have some properties essentially, these sorites arguments cast the existence of familiar objects in doubt. More commonly, philosophers worry that sorites arguments cast doubt on the reality of familiar objects by striking at the very bulk and body of those objects: the "sorites of decomposition" (Unger 1979a) seems to show that if objects of familiar size can be trees and humans, so too can objects of microscopic dimensions—which clearly would mean that nothing can be a tree or a human. In chapter 6 I focus on sorites paradoxes of the latter sort. I argue that the apparent susceptibility of familiar objects to such paradoxes does not impugn their reality; that we should, on the contrary, deny familiar objects a place in ontology if they did *not* appear susceptible to such paradoxes; and that the apparent susceptibility to sorites paradoxes need not be taken as real. We can dispel the appearance by endorsing the "degrees of truth" approach to vagueness. I do not offer a defense of this approach against the various objections that face it, but I do point out that it seems not at all an ad hoc trick when used to block "the sorites of decomposition."

Now for the causal exclusion arguments against mental causation.

4.1   Why Mental Causation Seems to Be Excluded

James decides that the best price today on pork chops is at Supermarket S, then James makes driving motions for twenty minutes, then James's car enters the parking lot at Supermarket S. Common sense supposes that the stages in this sequence may be causally connected, and that the pattern is commonplace: James's belief (together with his desire for pork chops) causes bodily behavior, and thereby causes a change in James's location. But many philosophers worry that such apparent mental causation is illusory (see, e.g., Heil and Mele 1993; or Macdonald and Macdonald 1995). Their worry stems from the close relation that evidently exists between James's arriving at the supermarket and an extremely complex event involving an enormous array of physical microparticles. This relation is in part a matter of co-location in space and time: exactly where and when James arrives by car at the supermarket, there and then do billions and billions of microparticles undergo billions and billions of motions and state changes. But the relation appears to be more than *just* co-location. It seems close enough, in particular, that whatever causes the extremely complex microphysical event, just there and then, thereby causes James's arriving at the supermarket itself.

Just what sort of event might be a cause of this enormously complex microphysical event? Another equally complex microphysical event, many philosophers reason, involving an equally enormous array of microparticles.

Quite possibly what went on in James's brain, when James decided about the best price on pork chops, is a large part of such an event: perhaps motions and state changes in those microparticles, given background circumstances including energy relations binding together the microparticles in James's car, sufficed to start a causal chain that eventuated in the complex microphysical outcome in the parking lot.[2]

But does this suggest that James's *deciding* as he did about the best price on pork chops did *not* cause his arrival at the supermarket? Some philosophers indeed discern no such suggestion. They maintain that the close relation between the complex microphysical outcome in the parking lot, and James's arrival at the supermarket, is simply *identity* (Davidson 1967, 1969). Similarly, these philosophers suppose, James's deciding and desiring as he did just *was* the complex array of motions and state changes involving microparticles in James's brain. So the thought that the microphysical event in James's brain caused the microphysical outcome in the parking lot hardly *imperils* the claim that James's decision caused his arrival; it *affirms* that claim.

But other philosophers do discern danger here. They worry that even if talk about James's deciding and desiring as he did picks out a complex microphysical event which, thanks to the laws of microphysics, was sufficient to ensure the complex outcome in the parking lot, such talk highlights features of that event that may have been causally inert. It may not have been *in virtue of* this event's instantiating mental properties, or propositional attitudes, that it caused what it did. James's mental life may enjoy only causal-efficacy-by-association—which would no more be *real* causal efficacy than guilt-by-association is real guilt (McLaughlin 1993). The impetus for this worry comes from the conviction that whenever an individual event *a* truly causes individual event b, the succession of b upon a must instance, or be underwritten by, genuine laws of nature (cf. Davidson 1970). Now it seems undeniable that there are genuine laws of microphysics. Perhaps no one law of microphysics ties the general *sort* of complex microphysical event that occurred, when the microparticles in James's brain all moved just as they did, to the general *sort* of complex microphysical event which was instanced in the parking lot. (This is actually a controversial question, and I will return to it in 4.4.) But even so there will be particular laws of microphysics which tie particular elements of that initial complex event to subsequent events, those in turn to others, and thereby ultimately tie elements of the initial complex event to elements of the complex microphysical outcome in the parking lot. And these laws of microphysics are precise and exceptionless, or as close to preciseness and exceptionlessness as any that nature will yield. In contrast, the only "laws" that tie decidings and desirings, such as those James did, to actions like James's betaking himself to Supermarket S, will be imprecise and hedged by numerous *ceteris paribus* clauses. So, if a claim to having caused an outcome depends on the lawlikeness of the generalizations that are instanced, the complex microphysical event that occurred when James decided as he did will, in virtue of being the *microphysical* event that it was, have a very strong claim to having caused the microphysical outcome in the parking lot—and with it, James's arriving there itself. In comparison, this same complex event in James will, in virtue of being the particular *deciding* (*and desiring*) that it was, have only a very poor claim to having caused James's arrival at the parking lot.

Beyond that, many philosophers think it strained and unmotivated to claim that the close relation between James's deciding and the complex microphysical event in his brain, or between James's arriving and the complex microphysical outcome in the parking lot, is really simply *identity*. The reason for *hoping* that the relation is just identity is the thought that thereby one can save the causal efficacy of James's deciding—and that thought seems questionable in any case. So, many philosophers suppose, one might as well adopt the more intuitive idea that the relation is one of supervenience. James's arriving at the supermarket *supervenes*, at least weakly, on the complex microphysical outcome; that outcome *composes into* an arrival by James. Likewise James's deciding *supervenes on*, rather than *is*, the complex event occurring in James's brain. There are events on different levels. But once James's deciding is explicitly placed on this supervenient level, its causal inefficacy seems even harder to deny. The complex event occurring (largely) in James's brain causes the outcome in the parking lot, and therewith brings it about that James arrives. The supervening decision by James lodges a weaker claim to having brought it about that James arrives. Can we credit this weaker claim—can we believe in routine causal overdetermination of human actions? The more defensible response, many suppose or worry, is to rule that the weaker claim is *too* weak. James's deciding causes nothing.

I argue in this chapter that this worry gets the real situation exactly upside-down. In fact the complex microphysical outcomes, which mental events seem excluded from causing, are not caused at all. For they are either accidents, in something like Aristotle's sense (Sorabji 1980, pp. 3–25), or coincidences, in a sense that David Owens has recently sharpened (Owens 1992). Each individual microphysical event comprised within such a complex outcome does have a physical cause; but it does not follow, and is not true, that the complex "outcome" event as a whole does. Mental causation, then, does *not* face competition "from below," from the microphysical level. Moreover, it may on its own level be perfectly genuine. For the outcomes that mental events appear to bring about—the motions of limb and larynx, and the changes in the agent's surroundings effected by these in turn—may have unified causal histories that the microphysical events subvening those outcomes do not.

4.2   A Suggested Analysis of Causation

Philosophers who insist or worry that mental causation is excluded by causation at the level of microphysics must suppose that the relata of "_____ is a cause of . . ." are fairly fine grained. They suppose after all that whatever qualifies as the microphysical cause of the complex microphysical outcome in the parking lot thereby also qualifies as a cause of James's arriving at the supermarket by car: the effects lie so close to one another that causing the former amounts to causing the latter. Yet as close to each other as they lie, there is a line of distinction so fine that it keeps them from being the same outcome. For it is the existence of an equally fine line of distinctness, at the opposite end of this causal trans-action, that keeps the causal efficacy of the complex micro-physical event involving James's brain from translating into causal efficacy on the part of James's decision.

Thus causal exclusionists must think of the relata of "_____ is a cause of . . ." as being states of affairs, or else Kim-style events—events with the structure, in the basic case, of object o's possessing during time t property p (Kim 1969, 1980). I myself agree that the relata of "_____ is a cause of . . ." are thus fine grained, and to this extent I think the exclusionists entertain a picture that is entirely right-side-up.[3] Where my disagreement comes is over two rather minor-sounding issues: whether "_____ is a cause of . . ." is agglomerative, and whether it is transitive.

But while the positions I take on those issues are controversial, the basic analysis of "_____ is a cause of . . ." from which I draw them is not, at least not markedly so. It is merely a modified version of Bennett's analysis in terms of NS conditions (Bennett 1988, ch. 3), and has elements in common with every main analysis currently on offer. There are to be sure differences between the analysis I favor and others currently defended, differences that can seem substantial the more closely one focuses on the array of puzzle cases, some of them quite fanciful, which has now become a staple of the literature. I will not undertake a detailed demonstration that the NS analysis deals better with those puzzle cases that really need to be addressed. If such a demonstration seems to be needed, please read this chapter as advancing a provisional claim: *if* a cause is a certain species of NS condition, *then* mental causation faces no competition from below. One could even think of this chapter as gesturing toward an "inference to the best explanation": this NS analysis yields a vindication of mental causation against causal exclusion arguments; we intuitively suppose that mental causation *is* genuine; so we should award a presumption of correctness to the NS analysis.

The basic idea then is that a cause of outcome e is a state of affairs c that figures indispensably in a set of circumstances jointly sufficient to ensure that e obtains. Typically a cause will not by itself compose all of such a set—that is, typically what qualifies as "a cause of e" will not strictly qualify as "the cause of e"—but will call on distinct circumstances, for example background conditions, for sufficiency to produce e. Also typically, the set in which c indispensably figures will be just one among several by which e could have been produced. So Mackie (1965) had good reason to describe the typical cause as an *INUS* condition of its effect, as an *insufficient but necessary* part of a set of circumstances *unnecessary but sufficient* to produce the effect. At the same time it is unduly restrictive to *define* a cause as an INUS condition. A state of affairs that by itself ensures the occurrence of *e*, and is all that could ensure the occurrence of *e*, should qualify as a cause of *e*. A cause is fundamentally an NS condition (a necessary part of a sufficient condition) of its effect.

Now for details. First, it is crucial that the set of circumstances in which *c* is a key ingredient has the right *sort* of sufficiency for *e*. If *c* figures crucially in a set of circumstances *logically* sufficient for *e*'s obtaining—or in a set that is, so to speak, *constitutively* sufficient for *e*'s obtaining—it will be counterintuitive to bill *c* as a cause of *e*.

Here is an illustration of the first sort of counterintuitive result. I go to the agora with the intention of seeing a play, and my debtor goes to the agora for an unrelated reason, and by accident we arrive at the agora at the same time—a lucky accident, since it results in my recovering my debt. Aristotle, from whom the example is taken, holds that the accident of our arriving at the agora simultaneously has no cause, and soon I will argue that he is right. But for now my point is that it would be counterintuitive to hold that our arriving simultaneously does indeed have a cause, and that it is caused by my arriving at the agora (as in fact I did) at precisely 4:03. For causes must be distinct from their effects. Yet my arriving at 4:03 *is* our arriving simultaneously—or rather is, together with my debtor's arriving (as in fact he did) at 4:03, part of a set of circumstances that logically amounts to our arriving simultaneously.

For the other sort of counterintuitive result, consider the complex surging and swarming of microparticles that composes into James's arrival by car at Supermarket S. Suppose that a crucial element in this sprawling microphysical event is the surging in a certain direction of so-and-so many carbon atoms configured in biochemical compounds, surrounded by so-and-so many iron atoms arranged in lattices that realize steel, all occurring at a certain distance above so-and-so many atoms of silicon bonded with other atoms in molecules that add up to pavement. The arrival of James's component carbon atoms in just that region should not count as a *cause* of James's arriving at the parking lot, again for the reason that causes must be distinct from their effects. *That* those atoms arrive in that region is, to be sure, a different fine-grained event (or a different state of affairs) from *that* James arrives in the parking lot. But their connection is still too close for the former to qualify as cause of the latter. The reasons for denying a causal connection here indeed go fairly deep. The whole worry about mental causation stems from the thought that the neural—ultimately, microphysical—states of affairs that compose into or subvene James's decision to go to S may really do all the causal work that James's decision appears to. But the causal work that the microphysical goings-on are thought to do does not include composing into or subvening James's decision itself. For their causal work is thought to be underwritten by the laws of physics, and the laws of physics do not quantify over decisions (Wittmer 1998). Subvening, composing into, is thought of as a *noncausal* relation between microevents and macroevents. Similarly noncausal then is the relation between the surging of James's carbon atoms and James's arriving in the parking lot.

A cause of *e*, then, is an indispensable component in a set of circumstances that jointly are *causally* sufficient—at any rate, not *logically* or *constitutively* sufficient—for the occurrence of *e*. It would be better to say this in a way which does not use "causally" in the definiens, and perhaps this is the way to do so: a cause of *e* is an actually preceding event *c* that, *in virtue of the laws of nature*, is an NS condition for *e*. (I am assuming that there are no *laws of nature* that tie macroevents of a particular familiar type—e.g., arrivals-by-car-at-supermarkets—to the fathomlessly complex disjunction of microparticle events, each of which would compose into such a familiar macroevent [cf. Fodor 1997]. This assumption should be congenial to causal exclusionists. For if there were such laws of nature, someone could say we should just *identify* the familiar [type of] macroevent with the disjunction of complex microphysical outcomes. Then decidings—such as James's deciding about the best price on pork chops—could likewise be identified with disjunctions of complex microphysical events,[4] and the apparent causal efficacy of James's deciding would no longer be *threatened* or *rivaled* by the efficacy of the microphysical event which composes into it.)

Two other details must now be considered: first, that something Bennett calls "the continuity condition" must be added to the basic account of a cause as an NS condition; second, that "the continuity condition" cannot, despite what Bennett says, supplant that basic account.

I toss a lighted match toward the top of an open gasoline drum, Bennett's example runs, and thereby top off a set of conditions jointly sufficient for the house's being in ruins an hour later. But my toss does not cause the house to be in ruins, for a bomb lands on the house at the instant I launch the toss. Its causation preempts that of the match (Bennett 1988, pp. 45–46). What the possibility of such preemption shows, as Bennett rightly notes, is that at every moment *between* a putative cause and its would-be effect, a circumstance must obtain for which the immediately preceding circumstance was an NS condition, and which in turn was itself an NS condition of the immediately following circumstance. When the bomb intervenes, it assumes the role of NS condition for the next momentary circumstance in the series leading up to the house's being in ruins, but the bomb's presence is not itself anything for which any stage of my match toss was an NS condition.

But Bennett also thinks that we can now drop the requirement that c be itself an NS condition of e, and let the continuity condition do all the work of analyzing c's causing e: it will be enough, Bennett says, that each intervening stage between c and e be linked NS-wise to its immediate predecessor and successor (ibid., pp. 46–49). This relaxation of the analysis, I maintain, yields counterintuitive results. For the continuity condition alone can be satisfied by the following sort of chain. P is an NS condition for Q and Q is an NS condition for R. But P calls on certain background conditions for causal sufficiency to produce Q, and Q in turn calls on *different* background conditions for causal sufficiency to produce R; moreover, the conditions Q calls upon get assembled later than the first set, and neither P itself nor the first set plays any role in bringing about the later set. Then so far as P's occurrence goes, it is a pure coincidence that somewhat later, R comes along. P cannot plausibly be said to cause R.

Consider, as illustration, this lovely example from David Owens (1992, pp. 18–19). I contract a disease that will kill me in six months unless treated with drug A. But so noxious are A's side effects that A itself will, unless counteracted, kill me within a year. Desperate, I take A. After nine months someone discovers drug B, which suppresses A's side effects—but only for two years, at which point the patient at length succumbs. I then take drug B, and two years after the original diagnosis, I am still alive. What causes me, two years after the original diagnosis, to be free from the clutches of death? Not that I took drug A, Owens maintains. On the contrary: it is mere coincidence that two years after taking A, I am still alive. I think this verdict is correct, though for slightly different reasons from those Owens gives.[5]

The central question is whether my taking drug A played a necessary part in a set of events *sufficient*, given the circumstances, for my being alive *today*. The answer is No. The set of circumstances in which my taking drug A played a part—the set my ingestion of A then engaged for its sufficiency to keep me alive nine months longer—included no circumstances at all connected with the development of drug B. Circumstances that would ensure development of B may then have obtained. But they were not causally involved in my living on for nine months more. Thus my taking A was not an NS condition of my being alive today—even though it was an NS condition of my being alive nine months later, and my being alive nine months later was an NS condition of my being alive today. So "_____ is an NS condition for . . ." is not transitive. Consequently, neither is "_____ is a cause of . . ."—a point of importance in 4.5.

4.3   How We Detect Causes, and Why an Accident Does Not Have a Cause

I have said I would argue that the complex microphysical mêlée that realizes James's arrival at Supermarket S must be viewed as either an "accident" in Aristotle's sense or as a "coincidence" in David Owens's sense, and that in either case it has no cause. Let me warm up for the needed argument by discussing simpler cases of what I mean by an "accident" and a "coincidence," together with the reasons for thinking that these simpler cases lack causes.

The joint arrival at the agora of my debtor and me can be viewed as an amalgam of two specific states of affairs: my arriving at the agora at exactly 4:03, and my debtor's arriving there at exactly 4:03. Alternatively, it can be viewed as a unitary, relationally defined state of affairs: my debtor and I arrive at the same time as one another. The amalgam of two states of affairs is an example of what I call a "coincidence." The unitary relational state of affairs is an example of an "accident."

My focus in this section will be on accidents. So let us ask what, if anything, brings it about that my debtor and I arrive at the same time as one another. My arriving at the agora when I did was the product of a background of intentions and decisions peculiar to me, and my debtor's arriving there was the product of a set of psychological background conditions peculiar to him. Was there some previous event that ensured that these two sets of background circumstances would yield up their products simultaneously? Did one and the same event figure indispensably in both causal chains, and figure in such a way as to make each chain yield its product at the same time as one another? If so, what would such an event look like?

To answer this question as carefully as we can, it is worthwhile to digress briefly to ask how *in general* we identify causes. How in general do we tell, of a particular event c that in fact preceded event e, that c was, operating together with background circumstances then obtaining, causally sufficient for e? The evidence that experimentalists in fact generally take as indicative of causal sufficiency, James Woodward has shown, is something called "invariance" (Woodward 1992). To understand what invariance is we must view events *c* and *e* as having structure. To pick a simple example, *c* might be a matter of object *A*'s acquiring property *g*, and *e* a matter of object *B*'s acquiring property *f*. (In the case where an object's acquiring one property causes *it* then to acquire another, object *B* will be the *same* object as object *A*.) "Invariance" is then the finding that as *A*-like objects acquire properties that contrast more and more sharply with *g*, relevantly placed *B*-like objects will display properties that contrast commensurately with *f*. In other words, values found in a *B*-like object of the determinable property which subsumes the *f* track, over a range of cases, values found in the *A*-like object of the determinable that subsumes *g*; the *B*-characterizing determinable reflects, seems tied to, the *A*-characterizing determinable; the *B* determinable fails to vary independently of the *A* determinable. Thus a low level of calcium in the diet is implicated as a cause of osteoporosis by the finding that, ceteris paribus, the more severe the porosity of the bones, the lower was the intake of calcium.

Of course it is fair to ask whether and why we *should* treat such "invariance" as evidence that *c* is, given the background circumstances, causally sufficient for *e*. The position on property identity staked out in chapter 2—namely, that any property's being itself is tied to its occupying the place it does in a range of contraries—appears to provide answers to these questions. For suppose that, in virtue of the causal laws that hold in the world, an *A*'s acquiring *g* *is* causally sufficient for a relevantly placed *B*'s acquiring *f*. Then that *B*'s acquiring *f* will be a causally necessary condition for the *A*'s having acquired *g*; if property *f* had been absent from that *B*, property *g* would have had to be absent from that *A*. But *what is it* for property *f* to be absent from that *B*? For *f* to be *present* in that *B*, on the position of chapter 2, is for that

B to contrast to varying degrees with other objects each characterized by one or another of f's contraries—by f' or f'' or f'''. So for f to be absent in that B is for one of these contrasts to fail to obtain. It is for B itself to contrast, to one degree or another, with items that do have f. In other words: the absence in that B of f is never an undifferentiated, all-or-nothing matter. It is rather a matter of the B's departing *to one determinate degree or another* from f-ness. And so too the absence of g in the A—which, we are supposing, would have *had to* accompany the absence of f in that B—will similarly be a matter of that A's departing to some determinate degree from g-ness, by coming to have g' or g'' or g'''.

But we are supposing it to be a function of the laws of nature that the B's departure from f-ness—had this occurred —would have had to be accompanied by a departure by that A from g-ness. We are supposing that a departure by the A from g would not merely have *coincided* with the B's departure from f, but would have *corresponded* to the B's departure from f. So we thereby are supposing that a *commensurate* departure by the A from g would have gone together with the counterfactual departure by the B from f. Had the B not acquired property f, and had it acquired instead the only slightly different property f', that could only have happened if the A had acquired, in place of g, the only slightly different property g'. To the B's having acquired the moderately different f'', there would have had to correspond the A's having acquired the moderately different property g''.

In short, selection by A-like objects of properties more and more different from g should correspond to—be found together with—selection by relevantly placed B-like objects of properties more and more different from f. This follows, given chapter 2's position on property identity, from the premise that A's acquiring g is causally sufficient (given background circumstances) for B's acquiring f. We should indeed expect the experimental findings called "invariance," if c, that is, A's acquiring g, truly causes e, that is, B's acquiring f.

But—to return from this digression—how can invariance help us with the case at hand? Here our task is to identify a cause of the *simultaneity* between my arrival in the agora and my debtor's. And simultaneity is a relation, not a property. Here "event e" has the structure "simultaneous {my arrival, my debtor's}."

Even so, it seems easy to identify relations that contrast at first just mildly, then more and more sharply, with the actual simultaneity between my arrival and my debtor's. That is, it seems possible to identify relations that are proper contraries to the actual simultaneity between our arrivals. We may imagine first my arrival's having been just a bit earlier than my debtor's, or vice versa; and then that one of us arrived earlier by an even greater margin, so that one of us nearly missed the other in the agora; and so on.

So if there was a cause of the simultaneity between my arrival and my debtor's, we now know what such an event would look like. It must be some event previous to our arrivals, such that variations on that event, first mild and then sharp, must seem likely to have gone together with arrival relations more and more different from simultaneity. That is: to identify a *cause* of the simultaneity of our arrivals, we must find some event that set up a *relation* between the various background circumstances which were causally responsible for my arriving at the agora, and the quite different background circumstances that were responsible for my debtor's arrival; and this one event must have played an indispensable part both in the former circumstances and in the latter.

Here is an event that *would* meet our requirements—if only it had occurred! Suppose my debtor and I had simultaneously heard the town crier announce that nuggets of gold free for the taking had been dumped in the agora. This event would have set up a *simultaneity between* the starts of two causal chains that led, respectively, to my debtor's arrival and to mine. It would then have brought other relations between me and my debtor into play, causally. Suppose, for example, that my debtor and I live equally far from the agora, and are equally fleet afoot. Then the one event of the town crier's shout would have been an NS condition for our arriving simultaneously at the agora. It would have topped off two sets of background circumstances, involving me and my debtor respectively, such that the two would yield simultaneity in the arrivals. (Or the crier's announcement could have started out the chain that led to my debtor's arrival later than it started my chain—my debtor lives out of earshot of the crier, but the cry was repeated by an excitable child—and then my debtor's being more fleet afoot than I could still have led to simultaneity in our arrivals.)

But ex hypothesi there was no such event; ex hypothesi the events and circumstances that got me to go to the agora were unconnected with, disjoint from, those that got my debtor to go. There *existed* numerous relations between my debtor and me, but nothing brought them causally into play. So our arriving simultaneously, like all accidents, had no cause. No previous circumstance causally sufficed for its occurrence. The causal processes of the world, to speak metaphorically, did not grab our joint arrival by its simultaneity when they pulled it into existence. Rather they grabbed our joint arrival at two different points, independently, and pulled: the simultaneity just came along for the ride.

Now, at last, for the microphysical mêlée that realizes James's arrival at Supermarket S. It too can be viewed as a unitary, relationally defined outcome: microparticles that compose into James's car move on top of microparticles that compose the parking lot at Supermarket S while simultaneously surrounding, between them, microparticles composing into James. This may not indeed be the way of picturing that microphysical mêlée which first occurs to one. It may seem more natural to view that mêlée as an amalgam of innumerable individual states of affairs, that is, as what I call a *coincidence*—that such-and-such a microparticle is undergoing such-and-such a motion at that precise location, while such-and-such others are undergoing precisely that sort of motion in precisely that other location, while yet another microparticle is doing such-and-such there, and so forth. But just as there is an objective question of what caused my debtor and me to arrive *at the same time as* one another, regardless of whether I arrived at exactly 4:03 and whether he did, so there is a parallel question concerning the microphysics of James's arrival at S. There is an objective question concerning, not what caused exactly such microparticles as were present in that parking lot to undergo exactly such motions and state changes as they did, but rather why *some* microparticles or other, clustered together in one of the ways that would compose into a car, were collectively moving above *some* other microparticles configured in one of the ways that would compose into pavement, while collectively encompassing *some* microparticles that composed into James.

But would this relationally defined microphysical development be just another accident—could it be said to have a cause? To find a cause for the simultaneity of my arrival and my debtor's, we looked for a previous relation-making event, variations in which would have gone together with variations in arrival relations. We had to identify an event relating my past to my debtor's, which when added (as a necessary element) to the background circumstances involving me and my debtor respectively, yielded a set sufficient for my arriving just when he did. This we could not do. But just so here.

For my opponent's aim, after all, is to use causal exclusion arguments to exclude from serious ontology James himself, James's car itself, and the parking lot itself. To prepare the ground for such arguments, he will have to operate *strictly* "from the bottom," from the level of the microparticles, to identify a cause for (what common sense calls) James's arrival at the parking lot. The question I have now raised is: what if anything caused microparticles composing into James's car to move above microparticles composing into the parking lot while simultaneously surrounding microparticles composing into James? The answer will have to identify some earlier relation-making event connecting microparticles in the first group to microparticles in the second and in the third—for example, that the microparticles composing into James's car *were* hurtling *toward* those composing the parking lot, while even then surrounding, collectively, those composing into James. This event will have to be such that variations on it can be expected to go with variations in the relative motions of these microparticles, and thereby with variations on James's arrival at the supermarket.

But are microparticles ever really influenced by such relations? In chapter 3 we noted that *individual* microparticles are almost never influenced even by the fact itself that they are contained in their host medium-sized object. In other words, it is almost never a necessary part, of what sufficed for an individual microparticle's moving as it did, that *all* the microparticles within its host medium-sized object were respectively doing such-and-such. Far less then are individual microparticles ever influenced by relations obtaining *between* that medium-sized object and *other* whole medium-sized objects. Are things improved for my opponent if she speaks not of *individual* microparticles but of *whole collections* of them—for example, of that whole collection that composes into James's car, or into James himself, or into the parking lot? But there can *be* such collections in the world only if there is something that unites their component microparticles. Now if there are in the world James and his car and the parking lot, what unites the component microparticles can be their *being located within the borders* of these medium-sized objects. But if those objects do not in ontological strictness exist in the world, then as we saw in chapter 3, nothing unites these collections. In particular, nothing determines which microparticles are included across counterfactual scenarios in, say, "the collection of microparticles that composes into James's car." So there is no fact as to how this "collection" would have reacted if differently related to other "collections." In sum: we just cannot turn relations between James and his car and the road into circumstances that will prove causally influential at the level of microparticles, if microparticles are all there is in the world. The microphysical mêlée that realizes James's arrival, if viewed as a relationally defined development, has no cause.

4.4   Why a Coincidence Has No Cause

Then are the prospects for finding a cause improved if we view that mêlée as a coincidence? A coincidence, in the sense

I take from David Owens, is a compound outcome that divides into states of affairs caused independently of one another (Owens 1992, ch. 1). That is, for any one of the component states of affairs, no previous development that rounds out a set of circumstances causally sufficient for *it* also rounds out a set causally sufficient for any *other* component state of affairs. The example given earlier is the case in which I arrive at the agora at 4:03 and my debtor arrives at 4:03. For the developments that got me to go to the agora are ex hypothesi distinct from those that got my debtor to go.

Following Owens I hold that no coincidence has a cause, but the position could be disputed. One might reason as follows. *Something* caused me to arrive at the agora at exactly 4:03, and *something* caused my debtor to arrive there at exactly 4:03. But then there is a compound state of affairs composed of these two NS conditions taken together, and it is as a whole an NS condition for the compound outcome of my arriving at 4:03 and his arriving at 4:03. The compound circumstance, say, of my conceiving at 4:00 a burning desire to see a play *and* my debtor's conceiving at 3:45 a languid desire to buy a bracelet caused the compound outcome that he and I each arrived at 4:03.

But I suggest that this reasoning assumes too casually that "_____ caused it to be the case that . . ." (or "_____ is an NS condition for . . .") is agglomerative—that if individual event P causes individual event Q, and individual event R causes individual event S, (P & R) causes (Q & S). The question "What caused the left front tire on my car to go flat?" undoubtedly has an answer. The question "What caused the Indonesian economy to collapse?" likewise has, let us allow, an answer. But consider: "What caused my left front tire to go flat and the Indonesian economy to collapse?" The answer, intuitively, is that nothing did. The outcomes have different causes. But if so, "_____ is an NS condition for . . ." is not in general agglomerative (cf. Owens 1992, pp. 11–15).

Now it does not of course *settle* whether causation is in general agglomerative, that intuitively it can seem silly to posit agglomerated causes. But it does make it fair to suspect that there may be some philosophically defensible position that rules out agglomeration. What might such a position be? It is held by many, many writers on causation that any true case of causing must instance some general law. I myself subscribe to this position—but it is not by itself enough to rule out agglomerated causes. For suppose that there is some general law of economics such that given financial conditions like those that obtained in east Asia generally and Indonesia in particular, an event such as the one we suspect of having triggered the Indonesian collapse would indeed be followed by massive devaluation of securities. Suppose too that there is a law governing the elasticity and cohesiveness of rubber such that an event like my tire's striking the sharp piece of glass in the road would lead to a rupture. If the conjunction of these two laws is itself a law of nature, the compound outcome that intuitively seems to have no cause at all may after all have had one. For it may have followed upon a compound economic-cum-automobilish event in a way that does instance a law of nature—an economic-cum-materials-science law of nature.

The crucial question then is whether conjunctions of laws of the world's workings are themselves, in general, laws. Precisely that claim is sometimes made. For it sometimes is claimed that all logical consequences of laws of nature—whether taken singly or in clusters—are themselves laws of nature (Lewis 1973, p. 73; 1986a, pp. 122, 126, and cf. p. 55).

In defense of our intuitions about agglomerated causes, I want to argue that this general claim is false.

For starters, then, note that in actual scientific practice, not just any conjunction of known laws is regarded as being a law in its own right. We may know of lawlike generalizations governing the evaporation of fluids, and of lawlike generalizations such as Boyle's law, and may wonder whether there are yet other, deeper laws that explain why both sets of lawlike generalizations hold. But in actual practice we would not consider such a demand for unification met by new laws that merely conjoined the generalizations we already know of. Such conjunctions would not be regarded as new *laws* at all. We would consider the two sets of generalizations to be explained and united by new laws only if we managed to enunciate laws that enabled predictions we were not before in a position to make, or enabled explanations of seemingly disparate phenomena we were not before able to formulate, or both. It cost real work, and conferred real benefits, to reduce the simple thermodynamics of gases to kinetic theory about molecules and statistical mechanics. This is not to deny that something *like* a conjunction of two known laws may *sometimes* amount to a lawlike generalization in its own right. If values of the antecedent in law L_1 sum together with values of the antecedent in law L_2 in distinctive and repeating ways— as when gravity and electromagnetism combine to shape the trajectory of an ion on the surface of the sun—then we will judge there to be a separate law governing conjunctions of values for antecedents in each of the original laws. But we will judge this precisely because the new law enables new predictions. What is sought in scientific practice when we look for a unification of cognitive science with neurobiology, or of string theory with the rest of physics, is not just a conjunction of lawlike generalizations already known.

Even so it is fair to ask whether and why we *should* be less than willing generally to allow conjunctions of known laws to count as laws in their own right—just as it was fair to ask why we should count invariance as evidence of causal sufficiency. Might there be philosophical reasons for holding that all conjunctions of laws of nature themselves are after all laws of nature? Or even for holding that *all* logical consequences of laws of nature are themselves laws of nature? To these questions, I maintain that the answer is No. But the details of the answer depend on the particular view one elects of the laws of nature.

On the "metaphysical" view, to use Barry Loewer's name for it (Loewer 1996), the laws of nature are ways the objects of the world are bound to interact with one another. (To put it metaphorically, they are ways the interactions of the world's objects are "constrained" or "governed" by the natures of those objects.) On this picture, what should we say about a case in which an expensive automobile tire runs over a sharp piece of glass on the streets of Djakarta, while at the same time the surrounding economy sharply reduces the value of that tire as a commodity—how do we explain that the automobile owner's loss has only a small value in the eyes of his U.S. insurance agency? May we see this case as an intersecting or overlapping of *two* "ways things are by nature bound to act"—as an intersection of the way rubber is bound to react to sharp glass, and the way an exchange value depends on its surrounding economy? Or must we see it as instancing a single, complex "way things are bound to act"—as instancing how rubber-commodities-in-a-collapsing-economy by nature react to adverse circumstances? It seems hard to see why we *must* give the latter answer. Where some object suddenly displays a value of the antecedent in law L_1 and a value of the antecedent in law L_2, it seems hard to see why we *must* say that that object's reacting as it does instances some third and different law.

On the "Humean" view of natural laws, the laws of nature are the propositional contents of certain sentences. One imagines a collection of sentences formulated in some canonical vocabulary that record all the individual events that ever happen over the course of the world's history. The law sentences are then those sentences that collectively best systematize or summarize this overall record—which together achieve an optimal combination of simplicity and strength. But now suppose that "L_1" and "L_2" are two such sentences. Will "L_1 & L_2" itself be such a sentence? What about "$L_1 \vee p \vee q \vee r \vee s$," where $p, \ldots, s$ are any indicative sentences whatever, expressed in the canonical vocabulary, whether true or false? Adding these logical consequences of "L_1" and "L_2" to the list of laws yields no gain in the empirical strength of that list, and seems to yield a new list less simple than the original. So it is perplexing that David Lewis—himself a prime exponent of the "Humean" view— held that all logical consequences of the laws of nature are themselves laws of nature (Lewis 1973, p. 73; 1986a, pp. 122, 126). It is true that the propositional content of many logical consequences of "L_1" and "L_2" adds nothing to the propositional content of the laws on the original list; many of the added law sentences would differ only in verbal expression from the law sentences on the original list. But if mere verbal difference is not enough to qualify such added sentences as *distinct* law sentences from those on the original list, it is pointless to insist that all logical consequences of laws of nature are *also* laws. If it does qualify them as additional law sentences, then that insistence is unmotivated, from the Humean's own perspective.

I conclude that there is no reason to suppose that, as a general matter, combinations or conjunctions of laws of nature are themselves laws of nature. So if cases of true causing must instance laws of nature, there is no general reason to regard agglomerated causes as genuine causes. We can honor our intuitive judgments that the compound outcomes that such agglomerated causes allegedly bring about do not have causes at all. We can and should agree with Owens: coincidences do not have causes.

But then if we view the complex microphysical outcome which realizes James's arrival at the supermarket as a coincidence—as an amalgam of innumerable microphysical states of affairs, each of which is caused independently of almost all the others—we will have to admit that that outcome does not have a cause.

4.5 But Is the Complex Microphysical Outcome a Coincidence?

Is it really true, however, that each individual microphysical event in the complex outcome in the parking lot is caused independently of almost all the others? Many of these individual states of affairs do descend from causal chains that overlap *at one point*. Some event within James's brain, which realized James's decision about today's best price on pork chops, triggered firings that triggered firings . . . that sent signals down James's motor nerves, which in turn triggered outcomes that triggered outcomes . . . that led to James's being present in the parking lot. At the level of microparticles, one movement or state change of a particular microparticle led to a movement or state change by a different microparticle, and so on. If causation is transitive, the disorderly microphysical outcome in the parking lot may not be a coincidence after all. For many different individual elements of this outcome may all alike have been caused by the same microphysical events in James's brain, when James decided as he did.

I have argued, however (4.2), that causation is not in general transitive. The basis of the argument is the claim that for *c* to be a cause of *e*, *c* must not only precede *e* but be an NS condition for *e*. It certainly can happen that event P was an NS condition for Q, and Q for R, without its being true that P was an NS condition for R. For Q may enlist different circumstances, in topping off a sufficient condition for R, from those that were enlisted and engaged in P's acting as it did. Exactly that is the case in the long causal chains that fanned out from the microparticle events in James's brain. Each successive motion or state change of a microparticle called on new surroundings and background conditions, caused independently from the previous surroundings and conditions, for its causal sufficiency to produce the next.

So the situation is actually parallel to one in which my taking drug A figures in a causal chain that leads to my being alive two years later, in another causal chain that leads to the manufacturer of expensive drug A being awarded a lien upon my estate, in another that leads to my winning a contest open only to people who have survived for seven months after contracting my disease, in another that leads to an article about me appearing in last week's newspaper, commissioned by a hard-pressed Features editor. That all four of these outcomes befall me is a coincidence, even though the causal chain leading to each overlaps *at some point* with the causal chain leading to every other. For no one previous development enlisted, in its acting as it did, a set of circumstances causally sufficient to produce each of the four outcomes. The only previous development that is even a candidate is my originally taking drug A. But at the time I took drug A *there were* no sets of circumstances causally sufficient to produce my survival to this day, or my victory in the contest, or the appearance of the newspaper article. These outcomes depended on background conditions assembled later, by causally independent processes. And that is enough to entail that the four outcomes are caused independently of one another. After all, "_____ is an NS condition for . . ." is not transitive.

Just so then for the innumerable microphysical states of affairs within James's body, and surrounding it, which realize his arrival at the parking lot. Many descend from causal chains that overlap at some point. But even these many do not have an NS condition in common. They are caused independently of one another. They do compose a coincidence. The compound outcome they compose has no cause.

5

Causes in the Special Sciences and the Fallacy of Composition

A mutation alters the hemoglobin in some members of a species of antelope, and as a result the members fare better at high altitudes than their conspecifics do; so high altitude foraging areas become open to them that are closed to their conspecifics; they thrive, reproduce at a greater rate, and the gene for altered hemoglobin spreads further through the gene pool of the species. That sounds like a classic example (owed to Karen Neander 1995) of a causal chain traced by evolutionary biology. But many philosophers believe that the causation here—the apparent causation, at least—is shadowed by causation exercised by one vast plurality of microparticles over another vast plurality, and by the latter vast plurality over yet another, and so forth (see Bontly 2002). They believe or worry that such causation at the level of microparticles preempts or excludes the causation that apparently occurs at the level of populations and traits and genes.

The key reasoning here is exactly parallel to the reasoning that suggests that mental causation is excluded by microphysical causation. The spread through this species of antelope of the altered hemoglobin trait seems very closely connected to an enormously complex and protracted microphysical event, involving a vast array of micro-particles, and coinciding in space and time with the spread of that trait. The connection seems close enough that any-thing that causes the spread-out microphysical event can be said thereby to cause the spread of the trait—assuming, for the moment, that there are in the world biological traits, organisms that have them, and populations through which they spread. The nature of this connection, these philoso-phers suppose, is supervenience or realization. The spread, they say, of the altered hemoglobin trait—assuming that this does strictly occur—supervenes (at least weakly) on, or is realized in, the spread-out microphysical event. And this spread-out microphysical event surely is the outcome, they suppose, of a causal chain that traces back to some equally vast previous microphysical event. Perhaps this previous event subvenes (or composes into) the very event that evo-lutionary biology identifies as what causes the spread of the trait. But even so it is a distinct event from that biological cause: it is a matter of many different microparticles' under-going many movements and state changes.

So there is causation at the level of microphysics, it seems, that at least shadows or parallels the causation apparently documented, in this example, by evolutionary biology. Nor do the philosophers who draw such a conclusion think there is anything special about evolutionary biology. They think that any causal transaction apparently discovered by any special science is shadowed by some causal transaction at the level of microphysics. This view, I believe, is what many philosophers mean by "physicalism"; in any case, "physi-calism" is the label I shall use for it. Physicalism so defined has a weaker and a stronger form. The weaker form— "modest physicalism," as I shall call it—holds that the causation apparently traced by special sciences is perfectly genuine, and that the objects involved in it exist in onto-logical strictness.[1] Such causation really is *shadowed*, not excluded, by causation at the level of microparticles. But because of the close relation between the outcome of any case of special science causation and the microphysical event that subvenes it—in our example, between the spread of the altered hemoglobin trait and the far-flung micro-physical event—modest physicalists must accept, it seems, that there is causal overdetermination of every outcome of causation anatomized by the special sciences. The stronger form—"hegemonic physicalism" seems an appropriate name—rejects such ubiquitous overdetermination, and argues that the causation at the level of microphysics sup-plants or *excludes* the causation that the special sciences appear to document.[2] Special-science causation is merely apparent causation. The putative objects that appear to exercise it do not—provided we take Alexander's dictum seriously—really exist, in ontological strictness. And then neither do the objects that figure in the outcomes of such causation.

Hegemonic physicalism is of course my target in this second part of the book. But in this chapter, as in the last, I shall focus on modest physicalism; if it is untenable, then a fortiori hegemonic physicalism is untenable. In the previous chapter I argued that modest physicalism is untenable as applied to the causation apparently traced by psychology and other sciences of human behavior, the causation appar-ently exercised by persons as thinking agents. That argu-ment focused on outcomes. Human decisions and desires appear to bring about changed relations of agents to their surroundings, yet the microphysical events that subvene these changed relations are, I argued, either coincidences or accidents—and either way simply are not caused at all. In the present chapter I raise objections against modest physicalism as applied to other sciences, and my argument focuses on causes. Now in fact the argument of chapter 4 *could* be extended to the *outcomes* of the causal transactions documented by the special sciences, for example the spread of the altered hemoglobin in our species of antelopes: these outcomes too could be said to be either coincidences or accidents. But a more striking problem with the causal transactions that modest physicalism sees as shadowing the transactions reported by, say, evolutionary biology emerges at the *cause* end. (It is one of these problems, moreover, that would complete the case for saying that there are problems for modest physicalism at the *effect* end as well.)

What has prevented adherents of physicalism from seeing these problems, this chapter argues, is the illusion projected by the fallacy of composition. It really is true that each individual microphysical movement, in the complex microphysical event that the physicalist identifies as shadowing the cause in a typical special-science transaction, causes some other microphysical movement. Perhaps ultimately, indirectly, each causes some individual movement (or state change) comprised in the vast microphysical event which shadows the outcome of that special science transaction. But it is fallacious to infer that the complex microphysical event at the cause end *as a whole* causes each movement comprised in the outcome, or causes them all together, or causes anything at all. That conclusion is unwarranted—and it is also, I shall argue, implausible in the extreme.

5.1 Identifying the Physicalist's "Causing Collection"

But just *which* complex microphysical event should the physicalist identify, as causing the complex event that subvenes the outcome of a typical causal transaction in the special sciences—for example, the spread of altered hemoglobin among our antelopes? I begin by noting that the metaphor of "shadowing" should not be taken too literally. *Which* microparticles, assembled together in *which* spatial groupings, between them start the causal chain that eventuates in the spread of altered hemoglobin among our antelopes—more precisely, in the complex microphysical event that *composes into* the spread of that trait? Physicalists may in fact usually assume that the right recipe for an answer is to point to all those microparticles, and only those, that are grouped together within the bodily boundaries of those ancestor antelopes in whom the lucky mutation first occurred. They may assume that to identify the complex microphysical event that lies at the start of the relevant causal chain, they should point to whatever microphysical goings-on occur just where, and just as long as, those ancestor antelopes gain extra forage, thrive, and reproduce at their unusually rapid rate. This would be literally to trace the shadow of the cause that evolutionary biology identifies.

But this recipe for identifying the microphysical *cause* event is not mandatory, and in view of chapter 3 appears to be naive. Any physicalist, even the most modest, should aspire, when confronted with apparent causation in the special sciences, to trace parallel causation at the level of microparticles *without quantifying over the objects recognized by the special sciences*. After all, what separates the modest physicalist from his hegemonic cousin is strictly the former's tolerance for causal overdetermination. In the story he tells about microphysical causation, the modest physicalist should say just the same things as the hegemonist does.

But what chapter 3 argued is that if one's ontology includes only the microparticles recognized by microphysics, and not also the medium-sized objects that common sense takes these microparticles to compose, one cannot hold that there objectively are in the world *groups* of the microparticles that occupy across times the same volumes of space as common sense supposes familiar objects to occupy. One cannot even suppose that there objectively is such a thing as the group of microparticles that *at a particular time* occupies just the volume that a familiar object occupies. For in the absence of familiar objects there will be nothing to constitute these groups as groups, nothing to set their membership conditions, nothing to make the difference between an individual microparticle's lying within such a group and its lying without it. Absent antelopes or persons or Max, there is no such property as lying within the boundaries of an antelope or of Max; at the level of microparticles, there is no such phenomenon as microparticles' being human-wise arranged. There is not even any property that unites the aggregate of microparticles composing Max the moment before his death; the members of that aggregate belong to it by virtue of their being numerically *the* very microparticles they are, not because of what, as microparticles, they are *like*.

So the physicalist should not be too quick to assume that the microparticles that participate in the vast microphysical event, which eventually brings about the spread of the altered hemoglobin in our species of antelopes, are all and only those that occupy the bodily boundaries of those ancestor antelopes. Certainly it is not *in virtue of* their occupying those boundaries that, in the eyes of microphysics, they act as they do; an individual microparticle virtually never is causally influenced by all and only the others in its host familiar object. Perhaps not even the microparticles that *in fact happen* to occupy those boundaries compose the full slate of microparticles in the physicalist's *cause* event. Perhaps other microparticles lying outside those boundaries were also involved. Perhaps—this actually seems likely—not all the microparticles lying within those boundaries were involved.

This caution should not be exaggerated, any more than "shadowing" should be taken literally. Surely the physicalist should say that *many* of the microparticles involved in the complex event that led, via long chains, to (the event subvening) the spread of the altered hemoglobin really *were* present just where common sense would say the ancestor antelopes lived. It would be an amazing coincidence if microparticles wholly remote from the particular ancestor antelopes, whose lives biology sees as responsible for the spread of that trait, had managed to produce a complex outcome just where that spread occurred, of just the right sort to compose into that spread. In pointing out the microparticles involved in the *cause* event—"the causing collection," as I shall refer to this plurality of microparticles—the physicalist should expect to be pointing *mainly* at places occupied by the ancestor antelopes. But the causing collection as a whole may be even more spread out across time and space, and more disjointed in setting and circumstances, than microparticles occupying just those locations.

5.2   Does "the Causing Collection" *as a Whole* Cause Anything?

Should the physicalist hold that the causing collection causes, in a single instance of causation, the complex microphysical outcome as a whole that composes into the spread of the altered hemoglobin? Or would she be better advised to hold that the causing collection causes *separately* each *individual* microparticle movement and state change that goes to compose that complex outcome? In the present section I shall examine the former answer, and in the next section the latter.

There is a powerful reason for thinking that the latter answer is the more promising, and it comes from the principle that every case of true causing must instance some general law of nature. I have announced my own endorsement of this principle (4.4), and *hegemonic* physicalists, at least, are required to endorse it as well. For when hegemonic physicalists are forced, by their unwillingness to allow widespread causal overdetermination, to choose between the causation apparently documented by the special sciences and the competing causation at the level of microphysics, their reason for regarding the latter as genuine, and the former as not, has to do with the laws that are instanced at the two levels. The laws of the special sciences, hegemonic physicalists remind us, appear to be riddled with exceptions unless we insulate them with ceteris paribus clauses—and so hard is it to spell out these clauses exhaustively that one suspects that one of them is "except where this law fails to hold." In contrast the laws of microphysics are precise and as close to exceptionless as any that nature will allow to be formulated. But this is a *good* reason for thinking that microphysical events (whether simple or complex) truly cause other microphysical events, while the events regarded as causes by biology or economics or psychology in fact cause nothing, only if true causings must instantiate genuine laws.

But given that principle, it is virtually impossible to maintain that the immense and protracted microphysical event, found roughly if not exclusively where the mutant ancestor antelopes throve and multiplied, genuinely caused the immense and equally complex microphysical outcome that composed into the subsequent spread through the species of the altered hemoglobin. Could there really be a law of nature to the effect that whenever such-and-such movements and state changes befall microparticles of such-and-such a description—the list of these being billions of places in length—other movements and state changes, again in the billions, will befall billions of other microparticles? The problem is not that such a law would be "general" in name only. It *would* be general in name only, of course. Any law that subsumed the antelopes' high-altitude foraging under a description as fine grained as this would assuredly come into play only once in the history of the world. (It would be "exceptionless" only in an empty sense.) Nor is the problem that, because antecedent and consequent in such a law would get satisfied only once in history, we could never have warrant for believing it to be a law. For plainly the idea would be that we were warranted in a different way in believing this. The idea would be that the massively specific law is a *theorem* jointly entailed by simple and familiar laws of microparticle causation—laws that, for example, link a movement or state change in one microparticle with movements and state changes in a few other microparticles.

The real problem is the one we noted in connection with agglomerated causes in 4.4: there simply seems to be no reason to suppose that theorems jointly entailed by familiar laws of nature—by laws whose status *as* laws is beyond controversy—are, as a general matter, laws of nature in their own right. They are not treated as laws in actual scientific practice, and no philosophical view on the nature of laws suggests that they should be treated as laws—neither the "metaphysical" view nor the "Humean."

It is therefore ill advised for the physicalist to hold that the causing collection produces, in a single instance of causation, the complex microphysical event as a whole that realizes the spread of the altered hemoglobin.

5.3 Does "the Causing Collection" Separately Cause Separate Elements of the Complex Outcome?

In 5.1 I argued that the physicalist should not unreflectively assume that the microparticles comprised in his causing collection are all and only those that lie within the bodily boundaries of the original mutant antelopes. (Nor should he assume that it is these microparticles together with all those that compose the succulent high-meadow grasses that the mutations enabled these antelopes to reach.) But to what question would this be an unreflective answer? Just what is *constitutive*, in other words, of a microparticle's belonging to the physicalist's causing collection—*what is it* for a microparticle to so belong?

The physicalist envisions the sprawling, protracted microphysical event that composes into the spread through this species of the altered hemoglobin. He imagines, for each individual movement or state change in this huge event, a causal chain that reaches back to the immediately previous microparticle movements that caused it, and thence to the yet more previous microparticle movements that caused those movements in turn, and which terminates in a microparticle movement found roughly—not necessarily exactly—where and when biology locates the cause of the spread. The causal chains will generally, if not invariably, terminate at individual microphysical events found where the ancestor antelopes were when they were prospering reproductively. To be the subject of the event at the start of such a causal chain is *what it is* for a microparticle to belong to the physicalist's causing collection.

Now consider an individual microphysical event o that figures in the outcome that composes into the spread of the trait—say, a movement in a microparticle M_o in the lungs of the just-born tenth baby of a granddaughter of one of the original mutant antelopes. Consider also the individual microphysical event that lies at the start of the relevant causal chain—for vividness, let us say that this is the movement c of an individual microparticle M_c in a molecule of nutrient that has just been transported to an ancestor antelope's stomach from its original location in a succulent blade of high-meadow grass. M_c is a member of the physicalist's causing collection. Mightn't the physicalist claim that the causing collection, *in virtue of* its component M_c, causes, albeit indirectly and via many steps, microphysical event o? Might he not in this way claim that the causing collection, in virtue of its other components, causes every other individual event in the complex microphysical outcome that subvenes the spread of the trait?

This is a far more promising suggestion than the one considered in 5.2. I now argue that it fails—but the argument requires some care.

What I am granting to the physicalist (for the sake of argument; cf. 4.5) is that microparticle M_c causes, via many intervening steps, microphysical event o. Of course this is a shorthand expression: what I am really granting (and what the physicalist claims) is that *something that happens to M_c* causes, indirectly, o. The cause is some state of affairs involving M_c, or some Kim event featuring M_c.

But should we grant on the strength of this concession that the entire causing collection, in virtue of its component M_c, causes o? Or, to unpack the shorthand, should we grant that the complex and protracted microphysical event *undergone by* the causing collection causes, by virtue of its component event c featuring M_c, microphysical event o?

The danger is that in granting this we will have given in to a misleading verbal trick. For we will have licensed the conclusion that the complex microphysical event undergone by the causing collection itself causes microphysical event o. Yet that conclusion may very well be false, or so we should suspect. For it is not in general reliable to infer that if event a undeniably causes event b, a complex event comprising event a together with event x likewise causes event b. Barry Bonds's performance in baseball in 2001, let us allow, caused the record book to be rewritten in a way that will stand for many years to come. It does not follow that Bonds's hitting as he did together with my publishing articles as I did in 2001 caused the record book of baseball to be rewritten for many years to come. It is in fact false that Bonds and I together rewrote the record book.

Precisely why the conclusion of such an inference is often false depends on what the correct analysis of causation is—although on any of the analyses currently defended, the conclusion will often be false. The analysis I endorsed in chapter 4 is (to simplify) that for event a to be a cause of event b is for a to be an NS condition of b. But was some complex, sprawling, protracted microphysical event involving *all* of the physicalist's causing collection an NS condition for o? The suggestion seems implausible at first blush, and even more implausible the longer one ponders it.

At first blush it seems clear that whatever the lines of causation were, that led from one mutant antelope's success at high-meadow foraging to the birth of his tenth great-grandchild, those lines did not embroil the entire careers of all the antelopes originally blessed with the mutation.

Perhaps the lines of causation were just those envisioned by biology, or perhaps they were really the ones that would be narrated by microphysics. Either way it seems clear that they involved only events in that one ancestor's career up to the time he sired the grandfather of his tenth great-grandchild, and not afterwards. They did not involve events in the careers of other ancestor antelopes, if any, in whom the lucky mutation also originally occurred. And even if the original mutation occurred in but a single ancestor, the relevant lines of causation involved only events in the life of the offspring of that ancestor who was to become the grandfather of that tenth great-grandchild. They did not involve events in the lives of every last *other* offspring of that ancestor—even though events in *all* these other lives *did* figure in the early success at foraging provided by that mutation. Hence the lines of causation leading to *o* did *not* run through some events that *did* figure in the physicalist's *cause* event. The lines did not embroil at least some microparticles in "the causing collection."

But let us consider the suggestion more closely. What *would* it have taken for a complex protracted microphysical event involving *all* of the physicalist's causing collection to have caused microphysical event *o*? How could that entire event have been an NS condition for *o*? What we have so far granted is just that the individual microphysical event *c*, in the one mutant ancestor's stomach, started a causal chain that eventually produced individual microphysical event *o*. So this causal chain would have had to follow a long and winding path. To it, every last other microparticle in the physicalist's causing collection would have had to make an indispensable contribution. Somehow that chain would have had to intersect the careers of (virtually) *every* microparticle in the body of *every* mutant antelope who enjoyed the early success at foraging which the mutation enabled. Indeed it may even have had to intersect the careers of every microparticle in every nutrient molecule in every blade of high-meadow grass, the consumption of which figured in this early success at foraging.

This suggestion is far closer to being laughable than to being believable. So it is, after all, just a cheap verbal trick for the physicalist to say that by virtue of containing microparticle M_c, the entire causing collection brings about individual microphysical event o. Thus even the more promising route fails to provide a defense of the claim that the causing collection as a whole causes anything. (A fortiori it cannot be claimed that the causing collection is a *common* cause of *every* individual event which, like *o*, figures in the microphysical realization of the spread of the altered hemoglobin. So that realization can after all be said to be, in the sense of chapter 4, a coincidence.)

Modest physicalism fails to be plausible for a typical case of causation that a typical special science claims to document. A fortiori, hegemonic physicalism fails to be plausible. So causal exclusion arguments provide no reason to doubt the reality of the objects involved in the causal transactions reported by the special sciences.

6   A Partial Response to Compositional Vagueness

A large part of what has, in recent philosophy, motivated many philosophers to question whether the familiar objects recognized by common sense genuinely exist is that so much about them seems vague and imprecise. If *real* objects must belong to natural kinds, *familiar* objects appear to belong to kinds having imprecise membership conditions— kinds that admit of borderline instances. If *real* objects must retain certain of their properties so long as they exist at all—if they have some of their properties essentially— *familiar* objects appear to have essential properties that sometimes are neither definitely present nor definitely absent. But even if one suspects that natural kinds and essences are merely structures we impose upon the real objects of the world, familiar objects can still seem to be barred from membership among the real objects, barred once again by vagueness. For familiar objects seem incapable of indefinite contraction: if a tree or a bicycle is reduced to the size of a single molecule, that tree or bicycle exists no longer. Yet familiar objects do, to most philosophers, appear to be compositionally vague. That is, it seems obvious to most philosophers that if from a tree or a bicycle a single component microparticle is removed, that tree or bicycle continues to exist. These two thoughts together yield a paradox.

The paradox is generated by "the sorites of decomposition" (Unger 1979a). Suppose we begin with an ordinary bicycle. Then if we remove from it a single component microparticle, a bicycle still remains, and that bicycle is itself a familiar medium-sized object. But if it is true with perfect generality that removing a single microparticle from *any* familiar object leaves that familiar object still existing, then removal of a single microparticle from this minutely reduced bicycle again leaves a bicycle in existence—and so on with each successor object as the reduction continues. At length we will have reduced the bicycle to something the size of a single atom, and will be forced to conclude that this too is a bicycle. But of course it is not a bicycle; the initial supposition must have been wrong: there never was a bicycle in front of us. There are no bicycles, nor any other familiar medium-sized objects (Unger 1979a, 1979b, 1979c; Wheeler 1979). So runs the worry.

In this chapter I focus on the vagueness, or rather the apparent vagueness, that generates the sorites of decomposition. I argue that there is a great deal of truth to the idea that familiar medium-sized objects are compositionally vague, but that the idea is not perfectly true. I then make the familiar point that if it is less than perfectly true that familiar objects are compositionally vague, sorites arguments are powerless to show that such objects do not exist (cf. Williamson 1994, ch. 4). I close with the less familiar point that the "degrees of truth" approach to vagueness offers immeasurably better prospects for defending the reality of familiar objects than does the increasingly popular "epistemicist" approach.

6.1 The Ground of the Appearance That Familiar Objects Are Compositionally Vague

Why is it very largely true that familiar medium-sized objects are compositionally vague? What is the ground of the compositional vagueness, or rather the simulacrum of compositional vagueness, that characterizes them? I contend that once we see the answer to this question, we will understand also why it is less than *perfectly* true that such objects are compositionally vague, and will understand, as well, why such a mincing distinction is not ad hoc but honest.

To understand why familiar objects have such compositional vagueness as they do, think first about what familiar objects would have been like if it were *false*—simply, flatly *false*—that they are compositionally vague. Or rather think, to use David Lewis's terminology, about *counterparts* of familiar objects in possible worlds maximally close to ours (Lewis 1986b). In other words, let us ask what objects would be like that were as much *like* familiar medium-sized objects as possible, *except for* their lack of compositional vagueness.

First, then, these would be familiar objects whose familiar properties supervened on what is done at the level of microphysics by their component microparticles. The characteristic hardness of a quartz crystal, for example, would still supervene on causal transactions between its component microparticles; so would the propensity of a tree to create nutrients for itself via photosynthesis. Now this is not necessarily to say that the familiar properties of such familiar objects would supervene on causal transactions in which *all* the component microparticles in the familiar object acted *in concert*. If the argument of chapter 3 is correct—an "if" to which I will return momentarily—this would in fact virtu-ally *never* be the case. For chapter 3 argued that an individ-ual microparticle in a familiar object virtually *never* exercises causal influence over *all* the other microparticles within that object, and virtually *never* is causally influenced *by* every last other microparticle in its host object. So the causal interac-tions that go to subvene the familiar object's familiar prop-erties will be fairly localized causal interactions. It still will be true that *between them*, the component microparticles subvene, by virtue of their several *local* interactions, the familiar properties of the familiar objects. That is to say: the familiar object can cease to have any one of its familiar prop-erties only if microparticles within it interact differently, in microphysical terms, from how in fact they interact.

Second, the familiar properties essential to the familiar objects we are envisioning would be tied together in pack-ages, by virtue of the way the world works. For that is how it actually is with the essential properties of actual familiar objects, as I argued in chapter 2. Hence any case in which one of our envisioned familiar objects loses one of its essen-tial properties will be a case in which it loses several.

Finally, then, suppose it is simply false that the envisioned familiar objects are compositionally vague. Then each such object can survive removals of individual component microparticles only up to a point. Beyond that point, remov-ing any one microparticle will bring it about that that object no longer exists—that a cluster of properties essential to that object no longer is present where just a moment ago the object existed.

It follows, by the point about supervenience, that once this critical point were reached, the removal of any single microparticle anywhere would bring about large-scale alterations in the causal interactions occurring among the remaining component microparticles. Indeed—since a number of familiar properties would all be departing in tandem—any removal of any one microparticle anywhere would bring about a number of large-scale alterations.

But then a familiar medium-sized object, reduced to this critical point, would put the lie to the thesis of chapter 3. Such an object would be so tightly organized, at the microphysical level, that the departure of any single microparticle anywhere would have large causal consequences on the behavior of virtually all the other microparticles in the object. Turning the point around, the causal interactions in which any microparticle in the object engaged, just before the fatal removal of a single microparticle, would depend on the presence in the object of all the other microparticles—including the one that gets removed, and this "one" could by *any* one of the others.

6.2   Objects Not Compositionally Vague Appear Vulnerable to Causal Exclusion

But then familiar objects of the brittle sort we are imagining would be exactly the sort of objects in which the causal exclusionists must believe, as we saw in chapter 4. They would be objects whose causal efficacy were rivaled at every turn by causation at the level of microparticles. For then there really would be, *at the level of microphysics*, such a phenomenon as microparticles' being car-wise arranged, or as their being James-wise or parking-lot-wise arranged. There really would be, *at the level of microphysics*, such a phenomenon as the microparticles' together composing a material parcel or lump exactly coincident, spatially, with James (or Max), with James's car, and with the parking lot at Supermarket S.

Then the nerve of chapter 4's defense of familiar objects, against causal exclusion arguments, would be killed. The microphysical outcome that composes into James's arrival at Supermarket S might *not*, after all, be an uncaused accident. For if microparticles within James's car are causally sensitive to their membership in that familiar object, they very well might be causally sensitive to relations obtaining *between* that object and James or *between* that object and the road or the parking lot. There might be a *cause* of the car microparticles' arrival above the parking lot microparticles even while surrounding the James microparticles (just as the town crier might have *caused* simultaneity between my arrival at the agora and my debtor's, 4.3). So there would truly be reason to worry that, because of Alexander's dictum, familiar objects of the brittle sort do not really exist, in ontological strictness.

Let us now return from these speculations. Almost everyone agrees that in the actual world, familiar objects are not thus brittle; they really are characterized by something like compositional vagueness (*pace* Markosian 1998; Sorensen 1988, p. 10). But now we can see *why* they are so characterized. They are so characterized because their essential familiar properties supervene on causal transactions that their component microparticles *between them* do, not on causal transactions that their component microparticles do *all in concert*. That is, what subvenes the familiar properties that familiar objects possess are localized microphysical interactions that their component microparticles engage in—interactions that do not depend on the presence in that object of *all* the other microparticles, interactions that exercise no causal influence on *every* last other such microparticle.

That is why the familiar properties essential to a given familiar object can go on being present—can go on being subvened—even if any single microparticle is removed from the familiar object. In other words, that is why the removal of a single microparticle, from a familiar medium-sized object, leaves that object still existing.

But at the same time, the familiar properties essential to a given familiar property must supervene on *some* microphysical transactions among the microparticles within that object. If *most* component microparticles are removed from a familiar object, that object's essential familiar properties must depart; the object must cease to exist. The microparticles within a familiar object are, as subvenors of its familiar properties, causally loose knit, and this looseness of knit explains *both* why the object *can* survive departure of any one microparticle and why it *cannot* survive the loss of a great many.

But such looseness of knit does not seem a paradoxical or unbelievable feature of familiar objects; on the contrary, it seems entirely believable, and itself almost familiar. (Recall how unsurprising my response in 3.3 to the objection about the billiard ball seemed to be.) How then can it entail a paradoxical or unbelievable consequence? It does entail, I have just said, that any familiar object can survive the departure of a single component microparticle. How then can that consequence in turn license a sorites argument, and yield the paradoxical consequence that the familiar object, which originally we think of as characterized by causal looseness of knit, is not characterized by anything since it does not exist?

6.3 Degrees of Truth as Qualifying the Compositional Vagueness of Actual Familiar Objects

The answer, I suggest, again lies in the *way* the familiar object's essential properties supervene on what is done, at the level of microphysics, by its component microparticles. They supervene on *loose-knit* causal interactions done by these microparticles—interactions that the microparticles do between them, but not in concert. But supervene they do. So it cannot be perfectly true that, as a general matter without qualification, removal of any one component microparticle leaves the essential properties still present—leaves the familiar object still existing. The idea that a familiar object is compositionally vague must have a great deal of truth, but cannot be perfectly true.

If the general thesis of compositional vagueness is less than perfectly true, then, so will substitution instances of that general thesis be less than perfectly true. "If *B* is a bicycle, then *B-minus-one-microparticle* is a bicycle" will be less than perfectly true. Then even if its antecedent is perfectly true, its consequent may be less than perfectly true. Similarly, "if *B-minus-one-microparticle* is a bicycle, then *B-minus-two-microparticles* is a bicycle" will be less than perfectly true. It may join an antecedent that falls just short of perfect truth to a consequent that falls short by a slightly greater margin. And if we conjoin a huge series of such conditionals, and treat material implication as transitive—which is just what a "sorites of decomposition" argument does—we may at length arrive at a detached consequent which is *false*. "*B-reduced-to-a-single-molecule* is a bicycle" can then be simply false.

There is, therefore, a way of admitting that familiar objects such as bicycles can (if real at all) survive the loss of a single microparticle, without having to concede that bicycles can be shrunk to the size of a single molecule—and hence without having to deny that there are bicycles in the first place. It requires merely the idea that statements about familiar objects need not be true or false simpliciter, but can be true to a greater or lesser degree, and shade off gradually into falsehood.

6.4   Degrees of Truth versus Epistemicism

Thus the defense of familiar objects that I offer, against the sorites of decomposition, relies on a general strategy that is already familiar (Williamson 1994, ch. 4; Keefe 1999). It is familiar that "degrees of truth" can be used to resist sorites arguments of various kinds. One can, for example, hold that it is not *perfectly* true that if a man is rich, reducing his wealth by a penny leaves him rich still, and thus can avoid a sorites that would yield the conclusion that even a man who has only two cents is rich, if anyone is; so likewise for sorites arguments about baldness, tallness, or heaps. But familiarity here is as much a curse as a blessing. It is well known that *all* familiar ways of responding to sorites arguments face substantial objections. I will not undertake here to discuss the objections—the worst of them concerns truth functionality—against the "degrees of truth" approach.[1] I will say only that however substantial the objections may appear, "degrees of truth" offers us the brightest prospects for preserving familiar medium-sized objects in our ontology. And preserve them we must, as chapter 8 will argue.

Many readers, I realize, will suppose that the "epistemicist" approach to vagueness offers at least equally bright prospects for preserving familiar objects. "Epistemicism" holds that as we run through the sorites taking pennies from a rich man, or the sorites removing individual microparticles from a bicycle, we *do* reach a precise point at which subtracting just a single penny more will render the rich man rich no longer, and removing a single microparticle more will destroy the bicycle (Markosian 1998; Sorensen 1998,

p. 275, or 1988, p. 10; cf. Williamson 1994). We merely do not know, the epistemicist says, where this precise point lies. But what 6.2 and 6.3 have argued is that this is precisely the picture of a bicycle, or of any other familiar object, that plays directly into the hands of causal exclusion arguments. If epistemicism saves familiar objects for serious ontology, it save them only to be destroyed by causal exclusion. So I hold to my claim: some version of the "degrees of truth" position must be defensible, since in all likelihood the truth of this position is required by the claim that some familiar objects exist, and that is a claim to which we simply are forced to subscribe (chapter 8).

III

Toward a Robust
Common-sense
Ontology

Artifacts and Other Copied Kinds

Suppose that a carpenter shapes pieces of wood and arranges them together so as to compose a desk. In ontological strictness, what has happened? Is it just that certain pieces of wood or bundles of cellulose fibers have gotten arranged differently toward one another, or has some object different in kind from either the pieces or the bundles been created? Suppose that the desk gets crushed, perhaps by a collapsing roof, and no longer can function as a desk. Is this just a matter of certain objects' being set in a new arrangement—perhaps very *small* objects, for example, cellulose *molecules*, if the crushing is severe—or is it a matter of some one object's being destroyed?

Many, many contemporary metaphysicians (as we have noted) find it hard enough to believe that even the pieces of wood out of which the carpenter fashions the desk really exist in ontological strictness. For even the pieces of wood appear to give rise to the worries about causal exclusion and about compositional vagueness, worries that were addressed in part II. The pieces of wood may also seem subject to "the problem of coinciding objects," to which I will offer a response in this chapter. But even readers satisfied by the responses I have offered to causal exclusion and vagueness, and willing to accept a promissory note about coinciding objects, may well balk at the idea that in addition to the pieces of wood there exists, in ontological strictness, the desk. It seems quite a further step to believe that an assemblage of wood pieces produced by the carpenter's intentional activity is a new object in its own right. The intentions of the artisans among us, and the uses to which the rest of us put their products, simply seem to play too lightly over the surfaces of our material surroundings. It can seem unbelievable that matter upon which such intentions and uses are focused thereby comes to be a material object different in its essential nature from what would exist in its place, in the absence of such focusing.

For this reason (and others) it is widely agreed that in the world that serious ontology inventories, there are no artifacts. Artifacts exist only in what Sellars (1963) called "the manifest image." Their careers are projected by people onto indifferent materials.

This chapter argues that, to the contrary, an artifact free ontology is unnecessary and probably incoherent. Artifacts—at least many artifacts—are, in ontological strictness, objects different in kind from whatever composes them. The essential properties that characterize (many) kinds of artifacts cluster together in just as mind-independent a way as do the essential properties that characterize members of familiar natural kinds—from argon atoms and H_2O molecules to glaciers and geodes. In consequence these properties are validated *as* essential, by the test of flanking uniformities, just as the properties of these more familiar natural kinds are. It is true that the *reason* for the clustering is different in the case of the kinds to which (many) artifacts belong—I shall call these "copied kinds"—from what it is in the case of the natural kinds usually discussed. In the case of the natural kinds usually discussed, the characteristic properties accompany one another in instance after instance, sample after sample, because of a common physical composition or microstructure. In the case of copied kinds, the properties essential to the kind accompany one another in instance after instance because of a common history of function (Elder 1995, 1996). The sameness in the instances stems from their surroundings, not from their insides. But the clustering of the properties is just as genuine and just as mind-independent. It generates just as positive a verdict from the test of flanking uniformities.

This chapter will attempt to show, then, that (many) artifacts have no *worse* a claim to being genuine objects than do many familiar medium- and large-sized objects—for example, geodes, glaciers, hailstones. It will address opponents willing to suppose that some such familiar objects really exist in the world—perhaps because they regard my responses to causal exclusion and to vagueness as plausible, perhaps because they have devised responses of their own; perhaps willing to trust in my promissory note on coinciding objects, or perhaps already possessed of a solution. Where the opponents whom this chapter addresses disagree with me is in holding that the careers of artifacts, their existences, are mere projections by people onto objects that include no artifacts. I thus take my audience to agree with me that there are in the world people, that is, human beings. My opponents can afford to believe this, I shall suppose, even though human beings themselves are subject to the two worries I have already addressed and to the third on which I issue a promissory note. Should my opponents suppose that human beings compose a natural kind unto themselves—more generally, that biological species are natural kinds? That is a

question to which, later in this chapter, I shall give a positive answer.

So the position this chapter attacks is strictly *projectivism
with respect to artifacts*. This chapter will locate the weakness
of this position not where many contemporary metaphysicians would—in its affirming the reality of us projectors—
but rather in a problem concerning the causes of our alleged
projection. To the naive question "What gets us to believe
that there are artifacts in the world around us?" the naive
answer is that our interactions with artifacts themselves do
this—we make artifacts, we use them, we observe them. To
the less naive question "If strictly there are no artifacts in the
world, what then causes us to believe in them?," the natural
answer would be that our culture or conventions or customs
do this; belief in artifacts is instilled by the sentences we hear
at our mother's knee. But a true projectivist must be careful,
in formulating an answer to this less naive question, to cite
as acting upon us only such objects as are recognized by his
artifact-free ontology. Quite possibly these objects do *not*
include such things as customs or sentences at all. What
objects *are* included? Let us allow that the projectivist recognizes all manner of *non*artifactual familiar objects, and
recognizes people as well. Even so there is, I shall argue, a
great gulf fixed between any answer to our less naive question that is available to a true projectivist, and the kind of
answer that seems natural. For the realm of our culture, our
conventions, and our language is bristling with copied
kinds. Thus if the projectivist offers an answer rich enough
to depict the action on us of items in this realm, he concedes
that members of at least some copied kinds really act and
really exist. Then he has no principled way of denying that
at least some artifacts exist. If on the other hand the projectivist denies that there are in the world any copied kinds,

he denies that there are any objects which might plausibly be said to cause, by their action on us, the projection he believes in.

Strictly speaking, this chapter is an ontological vindication not directly of artifacts, but of copied kinds. Copied kinds *include* many kinds of artifacts, but more besides: kinds of biological devices, kinds of naturally selected behaviors (e.g., mating dances), kinds of customary performances (e.g., rain dances), and kinds of linguistic structure. Kinds of artifacts picked out by the sortals of ordinary language often amount to copied kinds, but not invariably: chairs do not compose a copied kind, and neither do neckties or nose rings (see 7.3). I will be content if I have staked out a place in ontology for at least *some* artifacts.

7.1   The Sorts of Properties That Essentially Characterize Copied Kinds

Artifacts do have a place in ontology if, in fashioning a desk, a carpenter does not merely set pieces of wood or bundles of cellulose into a different arrangement toward one another, but brings a new object into existence. So too do they have a place if, when the desk is crushed by a collapsing roof, what happens is not just that the pieces or the bundles get arranged differently again, but also that something is destroyed. But just what marks the difference between "substantial change," that is, change involving creation or destruction, and "accidental change," change involving mere alteration? Verbally the answer is easy: an object undergoes substantial change if and only if the properties that are lost (or acquired) jointly compose an essential nature. But just what would the essential properties of artifacts be? And how would we tell that they are essential?

My contention is that the artifacts that do have a place in ontology are just those that fall into one or another "copied kind." Let me therefore begin with the broader question of what the essential properties are that characterize any copied kind. First, the members of any copied kind are characterized by a particular qualitative make-up or "shape." This will *literally* be a shape in the case of artifacts or biological devices, for example, the household screwdriver or the double-lensed eye of the eagle; it will be a shape somewhat metaphorically in the case of reproduced behavior, for example, the mating dance of the stickleback fish or a ritual rain dance performed by a particular human culture; it will be a "shape" in a purely metaphorical sense in the case of linguistic forms or constructions, such as the indicative mood in a particular language. Second, the members of any copied kind are characterized by what Ruth Millikan calls a "proper function" (Millikan 1984, chs. 1 and 2, cf. forthcoming a). That is, the members are produced by a process or mechanism which copies them from previous members similarly shaped, and does so as a causal consequence of performances, by those previous members, of certain functions—productions by them of certain effects. The process is, in other words, such as to produce more copies of previous items that produced such effects than of previous items that produced *no* such effects, or more copies of items that produced a particular such effect *more often* than of different items that produced it less often, or more copies of items that produced a *more wide-ranging* such effect than of different items that produced one less wide-ranging. In consequence there is, in a historical sense, something that members of a copied kind are "for" doing, something current members are "supposed to" do.[1] Third, the members of any copied kind are characterized by what one might call a "historically proper placement."[2] That is, the operations by past members, on which production of the current ones causally depends, were *co*operations with members of specific *other* copied kinds located alongside those past members. Past double-lensed eyes, in eagles long since dead, did something that causally contributed to the replication of eyes just like them in the eagles of today, but this "something" would not have helped eagles, nor contributed to the replication, if the eyes had not been accompanied by brains equipped to read the complex neural signals that the eyes sent. Screwdrivers have served to fasten objects together, but only because environed by screws suitably slotted and shaped.

Since "copied kinds" is my own coinage, I can simply stipulate that the members of any copied kind are uniformly characterized by a particular shape, a particular proper function, and a particular historical placement. But it does not follow that I can simply stipulate that the members of any copied kind are *essentially* characterized by three such properties. On the contrary my position is, as I have said in the introduction, that we must *learn* which of an object's properties are essential to it; claims of essentialness must be based on evidence. What sort of evidence, then, supports the claims I am making about the essential properties of any copied kind?

A conventionalist might answer that we learn which properties are essential to a given copied kind largely by tuning in to our own conventions for reidentifying kinds of artifacts and kinds of biological devices. We imagine, ensconced in our armchairs, various scenarios both realistic and not-so-realistic, and ask ourselves whether the items envisioned in them would still be household screwdrivers or eagles' eyes or stickleback mating dances. In the process we come to sense that it is our convention to individuate artifact kinds and biological device kinds by a combination of a specific "shape" and a specific performance that members of that kind are supposed to do. Thus for the conventionalist shape and proper function get welded together, as elements of an essential nature, by our ways of thinking about the world. Empirical discovery about how the world works—specifically, about how the copying mechanisms work that produce members of such kinds—then teaches us that yet a third property is attached to these essential natures, namely, historically proper placement.

But on a realist understanding of what it is for properties to be essential, *all* properties comprised in an essential nature must get joined together by virtue of the way the world works. The world must weld together the distinctive package of properties found in member after member of a given natural kind. There need be no single property responsible for all the others, no single property found among members of no other kind in nature (see 2.2)—no, the properties essential to a given kind may individually be rather commonplace, individually found among members of various kinds—but it must be a function of the way the world works that around some pair (or triad, etc.) of such commonplace properties enough other properties cluster to yield a combination found in no other kind in nature. It cannot just be a function of how we think of the members of a copied kind that throughout its membership a particular shape is joined to a particular proper function. It must be a function of the copying process itself that produces the members of that kind, that in all such members a shape is joined to a function and to a historically proper placement, and quite possibly to a range of further properties as well, in such a way as to yield a cluster of properties found in no other kind in nature.

Now the properties essential to any copied kind typically *will* be properties that individually are "commonplace," capable of showing up in members of other copied kinds. The mating dance of the stickleback fish has the proper function of inducing female conspecifics to engage in reproductive behavior—in the case of sticklebacks, this means releasing eggs—and this proper function is in fact found in a wide range of other mating dances and behaviors. The "shape" of the stickleback's dance, its choreography, certainly *could* be found in copied behaviors selected for a different proper function, even if in fact no such other behaviors have yet gotten selected; it could be the shape of a threat display, for example.

But such commonplace properties can be *essential* properties of a copied kind nevertheless, if the way the world works—specifically, the way the copying mechanisms work that produce members of that kind—is such as to ensure that whenever a pair (or a triad, etc.) of the properties that uniformly characterize that kind are present, other characteristic properties will likewise be present, yielding an overall combination found in no other kind in nature. The nature of the copying process thus must make the combination of a particular proper function and a particular shape be a sufficient condition for the presence of a particular historically proper placement. Or else it must be such that *that* shape in a copied dance and *that* historically proper placement for the copying ensure that the dance had *that* proper function. Or else it must be such that *that* historically proper placement and *that* particular proper function are jointly a sufficient condition for—could have been present only if there had been—the presence of just *that* shape in the dance.

How in general can one *tell* that the combination of two properties, wherever yielded by the world's workings, is a

sufficient condition for yet a third property? The test of
flanking uniformities (2.5) begins by turning this question
around, namely, as a question about a necessary condition:
how does one tell that for that third property to be absent,
in some closely similar kind, one or the other of the first two
would likewise have to be absent? The test then notes that
for that third property to be absent is for there to be a failure
of contrast with one or another of that third property's own
contraries. Thus the idea, that the absence of that third property would require the absence of one or another of the first
two properties, gets converted into the thought that a determinate departure from that third property would go with
an answering departure from one or the other (or both) of
the first two.

Thus in the case of a copied kind one would ask: would a
choreography differing from that of the stickleback's dance
in some one fixed way have uniformly gone with either a
particular difference in the historical audience of that dance,
or a particular difference in the function that led to its getting
replicated? And the answer is Yes. Among species other
than sticklebacks, dances differing in choreography *do* go
with correspondingly different historical placements—with
females in *those* species that are wired to respond with reproductive behavior of their own—if the proper function of the
dance is still that it is a mating dance. Among sticklebacks
themselves, dances differing in choreography certainly *could*
have gotten selected for and copied time and time again, *if*
they had had the correspondingly different proper function
of being threat displays, or if they had historically gotten
shaped by the presence of females correspondingly different
in their dispositions to respond by laying eggs.

Or consider the familiar household screwdriver. Does it
follow from the nature of the copying process that produces

members of this copied kind that *that* distinctive shape and *that* distinctive proper function together guarantee that the historically proper placement of the copying was an environment containing standard slotted screws? The test of flanking uniformities turns this question about sufficiency into a question about necessity: was that historical placement a *necessary* condition for that combination of shape and proper function? If items generically akin to simple screwdrivers had instead gotten produced alongside screws bearing a particular *different* sort of slot—say, a cross-shaped slot rather than a straight slot—would that difference have required, thanks to the nature of the copying process, a difference in either the shape or the proper function? The answer is Yes. In fact that very difference does go along with a commensurate uniform difference in the shape of the blade: that is, where the historical placement incorporates screws with cross-shaped slots, and the copying process still produces items with the proper function of affixing fasteners, it produces *Phillips* screwdrivers. Of course the same sort of copying process, in that altered placement, could still have produced items very similar to simple screwdrivers, that is, items still bearing flat blades—but only if it had happened upon a different proper function with which to endow those items. In sum, to the change in historically proper placement there really *would* (sometimes there *does*) correspond a change in either shape or in proper function.

In the case of typical copied kinds, then, the three features I have outlined are shown by the test of flanking uniformities to cluster together in just the manner of properties that jointly compose an essential nature. There is *realist* evidence for judging that any copied kind essentially is characterized by shape, proper function, and historically proper placement. Copied kinds truly *have* essential properties, then, in the same traditional sense as do any other kinds that occur in the world. When a collapsing roof crushes a desk, causing the shape of a desk to be present no longer, an essential rather than accidental property is lost; the collapse involves not just alteration, but the destruction of an object.

But so far, so little. If copied kinds had essential natures encompassing *only* three properties of the sorts I have indicated, they would have fairly uninteresting essential natures, and inductions over members of such kinds could yield little new knowledge about what their members are bound to be like. In the next section I shall argue that very often, copied kinds have essential natures encompassing more properties than just those of shape, function, and placement.

Still, even the identification of a core of properties essential to the members of any copied kind may help dispel some of the skepticism canvassed at the outset of this chapter about the place of artifacts in ground-level ontology. When an artisan fashions an artifact, he works on materials such as wood or steel or stone. As stuffs, these materials already have essential natures of their own. It can, as we noted, seem unbelievable—too much like magic—that merely by shaping and joining parcels of such materials in ways that reflect his intentions the artisan brings about the existence of a new object, one possessed of an essential nature not present before. But if the position of this chapter is correct, the creation does not begin with the artisan's intending what he does. Rather, the essential properties that his product will inherit stem from a history of function and of copying that began well before the artisan undertook his work. This history reaches forward through the artisan's motions—it shapes his shaping. Its existence and its efficacy are independent, largely or even entirely, of the artisan's will.

For similar reasons we should have no compunctions about terming copied kinds *natural kinds*. It is true that artifacts belong to the kinds they do by virtue of how we shape them—that is, as a reflection of our intelligence and agency. But we ourselves, with our intelligence and agency, are items that nature produced. So the kinds into which we make artifacts fall are kinds that nature fashions through us.

7.2 Further Sorts of Properties Essential to Many Copied Kinds

I now argue that around any actual combination of copied "shape," proper function, and historically proper placement, a number of other properties will typically cluster— enough properties to make up a fairly interesting essential nature. This is so whether the combination characterizes a particular kind of artifact, a kind of biological device, a behavioral routine installed by natural selection, a custom embedded in a human culture, or a linguistic structure. But before beginning to argue for this contention, I must say a few words to justify placing items seemingly so disparate under the common rubric of "copied kind." The justification rests on the idea that items of all these disparate sorts are produced by copying processes that, while differing in details, are alike in broad and important respects.

The differences admittedly catch the eye more quickly than do the similarities. The process that copied genes for double-lensed eyes, so effectively that they passed from lucky mutations in a few protoeagles to fixation in the gene pool of the eagles of today, was unsupervised and "blind"— it was natural selection. Natural selection may also be said, as I will presently argue, to have copied the eyes themselves in today's eagles from the eyes of ancestor eagles. But a competent craftsman who fashions a screwdriver, on the model of previous screwdrivers that have proven effective, copies consciously and deliberately. And between these extremes there may seem to be a spectrum of interestingly different copying processes. The current generation of an indigenous people may deliberately copy its ritual rain dance from the dances of previous generations, but with no clear understanding of the benefit to social cohesion, which is the real reason (let us suppose) for the dance's continued existence. An automobile manufacturer might stay in business only because its automobiles replicate the design of pollution-free prototypes developed by a competitor, but may thus design its automobiles out of concern for profit alone; the replication of a pollution-free design may be not unconscious, but not intentional either.

But there is a crucial similarity among the copying processes that produce these seemingly disparate items. They are all causally sensitive to the performance, by the past tokens that figure as "originals" in the copying process, of certain sorts of functions—perceptual or behavioral or physiological functions among "originals" embodied in animals, functions of fitting and turning and bending among "originals" embodied in tools, functions affecting performance and ease of use among commodities. The processes are such as to copy for a longer time, or in greater numbers, previous items that have served some such function than previous items that served none; or previous items that served such a function more often or more effectively than items that served the same function less well; or previous items that served a more urgent such function than items that served one less urgent. The copying processes or mechanisms are not confined by the ways they work to copying items of just *that* qualitative make-up found in the items *currently* produced. They will have copied qualitatively different items, to a lesser degree. Their histories will have warranted the claim that if originals *more* functional than the current products had historically been available for copying, those more functional originals *would have* gotten copied instead.

This is why it is indeed legitimate to speak of natural selection as copying, not just genotypic configurations from generation to generation, but also the phenotypic traits that express those genotypes. Directly, of course, it is only genes that get copied. The offspring of an amputee do not inherit wooden legs. But often what causes a particular genotype to get replicated more and more widely, in generation after generation, is not random genetic drift, but the adaptational (and hence reproductive) success of the phenotypic trait for which it codes. In such circumstances the consequent spread through the gene pool of the underlying genotype in turn causes a spread through the species of that phenotypic trait. Hence often, the successes achieved by earlier tokens of a phenotypic trait cause the production of later tokens. There is a process that produces eyes in present-day eagles that resemble eyes in ancestor eagles, and it is causally sensitive to the successes scored by those ancestor eyes. There is a mechanism responsible for the presence in present-day beavers of dam-building behavior, and it is causally sensitive to the successes achieved by past tokens of just such behaviors. In short, while what *directly* gets copied from generation to generation are genes, it is also true that *indirectly* phenotypic traits get copied across generations, copied as a causal consequence of functions served in the past. In just this sense the dams made by present-day beavers can be said to be copies of dams made by ancestor beavers; as Dawkins (1982) points out, the dam is as much a part of the beaver's naturally selected phenotype as is the beaver's tail.

Items produced by such success-sensitive copying processes, then, are the subject of my present contention. The contention is that where a particular copied "shape," a past performance causally responsible for the copying (i.e., a proper function), and a historically proper placement all come together, further properties will typically cluster with them. Inferences from examined samples will non-accidentally hold true for copied kinds, just as for natural kinds more familiar in philosophical discussions. These further properties fall into three main categories. There are properties connected with material composition; there are functional peculiarities of the design that is copied; and there are specific propensities for historical change when and if the proper placement should alter.

First, then, the members of a given copied kind can warrantedly be expected of be made of the right sort of stuff.[3] This is obviously true for artifacts and kinds of phenotypic hardware; it is true in a transposed sense for even repro-duced behaviors. Household screwdrivers, for example, can warrantedly be expected to be made of fairly firm materials. For the screws they turn must be firm enough to penetrate the materials to which they are applied, and the screwdrivers themselves must turn the screws without being bent in the process. The materials composing a beaver dam must be firm enough that, when woven together in the characteristic design, they do not snap or dissolve under the pressure of the impounded water. But they must not be so firm or dense that beavers cannot grasp pieces of them with their jaws. The mating dance of a particular species of fish must not have a choreography so acrobatic that almost no male can dance it, nor so complex that almost no female can recognize it.

Second, the members of any copied kind will embody a particular design solution to what might broadly be termed an engineering problem, and with that solution will go particular excellences and liabilities. The mechanism in humans for localizing sounds has a simple, "low cost" design, but a recurrent and predictable failing: it commonly fails to differentiate a sound emanating from a source 30° to 60° removed from "straight ahead" from a sound emanating from 30° to 60° removed from "straight behind." The stereoscopic visual systems found in mammalian predator species embody a solution to the task of achieving depth perception, but one achieved at the cost of a narrowing of the visual field. Human rituals involving sacrificial offerings embody solutions to the challenge of meeting social and emotional needs, but in times of famine predictably entail suffering and disruption as well.

Finally, the members of at least some copied kinds will have propensities to shift in their qualitative makeup, or a history of having actually done so, in ways that coincide with changes in their historically proper placement. The hunting behaviors in a predator species will alter as the customary prey species acquires new routines of evasion and escape, or dies out and gets replaced by other prey species. New strategies for responding to social defection may develop in a given population as defection comes to be more common. Mating dances or plumage may become more stylized and exaggerated in a given species, when females start favoring by their responses the more colorful of the dances or plumages originally on offer. The syntactically significant suffixes and markers in a language will shift as the phonemes of that language come to be typed differently by its speakers.

There are then reasons for thinking that copied kinds will be characterized by essential properties beyond those that form the core of their essential natures—beyond the properties of shape, proper function, and historically proper placement. Copied kinds will at least often have rather rich essential natures, just as is the case with the natural kinds more often discussed in the literature—for example, chemical kinds such as water, physical elements such as gold. But the scope of this point should not be exaggerated. Some copied kinds may have thin essential natures, and some may even be characterized only by a distinctive combination of shape, function, and placement. Even they will have genuine essential natures, as 7.1 argued, but natures that are certainly less interesting.

7.3 Classes of Artifacts That Are and Are Not Copied Kinds; Coinciding Objects

Let us now focus on the particular case of artifacts. I have so far argued that copied kinds in general are characterized by clusters of essential properties; thus that where the properties in such a cluster arise or cease to obtain, *substantial* change occurs; thus that members of such kinds exist in ontological strictness. But what follows about the ontological status of the artifacts that common sense recognizes? Is every kind of artifact for which there is a sortal in common usage—for example, chairs and tables and sweaters—a copied kind in its own right? If not, what marks the division between the kinds of artifacts that may be admitted to our ontology and those that must be treated as mere projections of our language and culture?

In this section I defend and refine the position that broad and inclusive kinds of artifacts are less likely to constitute true copied kinds than are kinds more specifically delimited. Chairs are less likely to compose a copied kind than are desk chairs, and desk chairs are less likely than Eames desk chairs of the 1957 design. But this is not to say that where one kind of artifact is a specific version of some broader kind, *only* the more specific can claim to be a true copied kind. Given a modicum of specificity, *both* may be perfectly genuine as copied kinds. The difference may be only that the more specific kind is characterized by a richer, more interesting cluster of properties.

The basic rationale for this position is obvious: kinds as broad as chairs and tables can barely be said to have any one "shape" or qualitative character in common at all. Moreover, they have no well-defined historically proper placement: there are dining room chairs, electric chairs, birthing chairs, and camping chairs. The challenge lies not in finding reasons for thinking that artifact kinds must be *fairly specific* to qualify as copied kinds. It lies rather in defending the claim that a fair degree of specificity is *enough*—that where one artifact kind is a specific version of another, the former need not always usurp the latter's claim to being a copied kind. For suppose that one artifact kind is a specific version of some broader artifact kind, that both do amount to copied kinds, and that some one artifact is a member of both. Suppose, to make it concrete, that some one chair is both a desk chair and an Eames 1957 desk chair. Then we seem to be faced with "the problem of coinciding objects." Exactly where that chair is located there is an object that essentially has the characteristic Eames shape, and an object that does not essentially have that shape. But if object A differs in its essential properties from object B, A and B are distinct.

So in that location there are two objects. Each of them is a chair. Yet if the 30-pound desk chair and the 30-pound Eames desk chair are both placed on a scale—which can be done, *mirabile dictu*, in a single motion—the scale reads "30," not "60."

The problem of coinciding objects has indeed been lurking in the wings since this chapter began. It is the main reason why some contemporary metaphysicians judge that artifacts do not really exist in the world (see Rea 1997). For artifacts of many familiar kinds can readily be supposed to coincide with matter-objects that differ from those artifacts in their modal properties. A statue of Goliath, for example, might be thought to coincide with a particular lump of gold; but this lump would surely be able to survive getting flattened, while the statue could not. It seems to follow that the statue, if real, is a distinct object from the lump. But the presence of these two objects in the same volume is undetectable by scales and other instruments of observation. Some contemporary metaphysicians infer that one of these objects must go, namely, the statue (e.g., Zimmerman 1995).

Now the problem of coinciding artifacts seems to me genuine, and I will return to it presently. The problem of coincidence between any artifact and a matter-object is another matter. Why need we suppose that there is some one "matter-y" thing, possessed of a spatiotemporal career of its own, which at present composes the statue, but may later not do so? Our ontology must, to be sure, admit that there is such a stuff or substance as gold; gold, like water and bronze, is what Aristotle called a secondary substance, one that by nature occurs in spatially localized quantities. Our ontology must also recognize the individual atoms that between them compose any localized quantity of gold, and the molecules that compose any sample of water. But why need we say that in addition to the one stuff of which a homogeneous artifact is made, there is some one object that composes that artifact?

Just what nature are we to think of such a matter-object as having—just what features should we think of as marking out its career? One answer sometimes discussed is that the object is the *aggregate* of gold atoms now within the statue. *This* matter-object by nature survives just as long as those very individual atoms continue to exist, and just where they come to be; unlike the statue, it can survive radical dismemberment, but also unlike the statue, cannot survive the destruction of even one of those atoms. An alternative answer is that the matter-object in question is a *parcel* of gold, defined by its having exactly that statuesque shape. When even a small chunk is clipped from Goliath's ear, the statue continues to exist, albeit in damaged condition, but the parcel is no longer.

There is a third answer as well, a more promising answer, and I will consider it in a moment. The problem with these first two matter-objects is that they are said to have, essentially, properties that do not test out *as* essential on any test of essentialness that is even remotely appropriate, provided we adopt a realist stance toward essentialness (Elder 1998a). Now if we adopt a conventionalist stance toward essentialness, things may indeed be different. It cannot be said that *people in general* wield conventions for reidentifying aggregates and parcels—for tracing their careers across space and time—but there are *philosophers* who coin and adhere to precisely such conventions. And then if it is true that our conventions are constitutive of essential status—if the features that our conventions take as cues for reidentification, whether of individuals or of kinds, eo ipso *are* essential properties of individuals or of kinds—then aggregates and lumps have just those essential properties that the present "problem of coinciding objects" supposes them to have. But conventionalism about essentialness, I argued in part I, yields an incoherent ontology. And if we adopt a realist stance toward essentialness, the only appropriate tests for essentialness must look to ways properties cluster together reliably—across all members of some class, even in counterfactual scenarios—in virtue of the way the world works. The test of flanking uniformities is one such test (and, so far as I can tell, the only such test).

But set the specifics of flanking uniformities aside. Could *any* test show that the properties essential to an aggregate of gold atoms, or to a parcel of gold, cluster together with other properties, in virtue of the laws of nature? Begin with the case of the aggregate. It essentially has the property, supposedly, of *being-composed-of-numerically-those-atoms-of-gold*. But could *being-composed-of-numerically-those-atoms-of-gold* engage the laws of nature in such a way that yet other properties will cluster together with it? No, since the laws of nature are never engaged by bare numerical identity, by haecceities. They apply to things by virtue of the things' properties or circumstances or relations—by virtue of repeatables. (The same reasoning shows that origin, i.e., being-derived-from-numerically-that-matter or being-derived-from-numerically-that-source, also cannot be essential; I will return to this point presently.)

Turn next to the parcel of gold coincident, supposedly, with the statue. It is said to have essentially the property of being of exactly *that* extent or size or mass. But, with rare exceptions such as piles of Uranium-235, that a sample of some stuff is of one precise size or another makes no further difference, under the laws of nature, to what other properties it has.

Then might we think of the matter-object with which
Goliath appears to coincide in yet a third way—as just *that
sample* of gold, that expanse or chunk of gold? The persistence conditions for this matter-object would be more
loosely defined than for either of the first two; they indeed
vary with different conversational contexts. Sometimes
asking "Just where is that sample of gold now? Does it still
exist?" will amount to asking whether 90 percent of the
atoms in the original statue are still joined together, sometimes just to only whether half or more of them are joined
together, sometimes just to asking whether some percentage
of them still now exist. My response is that all such questions are perfectly genuine. But they are questions about
many objects, in the plural—many gold atoms—not questions about some one object.

At the same time, the problem of coinciding *artifacts* does
seem perfectly genuine. Artifacts belonging to one copied
kind often do, it seems, exactly coincide with artifacts
belonging to some other copied kind—typically another
kind more specific, or less. An Eames desk chair, 1957
design, occupies exactly the same volume as does some desk
chair; and, as in Sidelle's example (1998), a single long piece
of woolen yarn, itself an artifact, might compose the whole
of a sweater. How then can two distinct artifacts—which
differ, after all, in their essential properties—be wholly
present at exactly the same place?

The sting of this question seems to come precisely from
the realist position on essentialness which I so vigorously
endorse. If essentialness is really *out there in the things*,
it seems, a thing must have essentially those properties
that *are* essential to it strictly in virtue of its own material makeup, its being composed of just *those* atoms. And
then if thing A and thing B have exactly the same material

composition, they cannot differ in respect of their essential properties (cf. Heller 1990, pp. 30–31).

But what this chapter has argued is that, in the case of copied kinds, essentialness can be *out there in the things* in virtue of the histories of function that lie behind the causes that produced the things. The long piece of yarn springs from a copying process long underway, continued over generations because of successes its earlier products scored at composing primitive socks and mittens and cords as well as sweaters; the "shape" in virtue of which it figures as product of this process involves its thinness and the crisscrossing of wool fibers within it, not the sweatery form it currently assumes. Eames desk chairs spring from a copying process that began long after the copying of *some* desk chairs *or other*, and that process continued because of special features unique to its products—their exiguous and sinuous shapes, their bright color, and so forth.

Because the Eames desk chair and the desk chair possess different essential properties in virtue of their different *histories*, and not in virtue of any difference in *material composition*, it is unsurprising that when the two are put on the scale, the scale still reads "30." The two are composed of exactly the same matter! Now true, this answer would prolong our difficulties about coinciding objects, rather than resolve them, if expressed as the claim that *the parcel* of matter which composes, for example, the Eames desk chair also composes the desk chair, or if expressed as a parallel claim about *the aggregate* of atoms that composes either. But it need not be expressed that way. It can rather be expressed as the claim that every atom found within the boundaries of the Eames desk chair is found in the boundaries of the desk chair, and vice versa. (Refinements may be needed to reflect the fuzziness of the boundaries of either object. But they reflect the fact that either object is compositionally vague, not the problem of coinciding objects.)

7.4 "Historical Kinds" and Biological Species

My position, in sum, is this. Commonly recognized kinds of artifacts that are very broad and inclusive are unlikely to constitute copied kinds; fairly specific familiar kinds of artifacts are all likely to do so (more on this in a moment); and among these *fairly* specific kinds the *more* specific will in general be the more interesting copied kinds, the ones that display richer clusters of characteristic properties. Eames 1957 desk chairs are a more interesting copied kind than are desk chairs in general. But now why is that, exactly? Ruth Millikan has argued that for the special sciences, "historical kinds" are especially likely to sustain a rich range of inductive inferences (Millikan 1999). "Historical kinds" are defined as ones whose members not only bear qualitative resemblances to one another but derive from numerically the same historical process of copying as one another. Are Eames 1957 desk chairs a richly characterized artifact kind because they all stem from numerically the same originals in the Eames's studios? Is it true in general that the most interesting copied kinds are historical kinds?

Millikan's contention seems to me to give distorted expression to an important truth. By speaking of historical *kinds*, not just *groupings*, she suggests that there would be a difference in essential nature between, say, an Eames 1957 desk chair and another chair qualitatively just like it that were derived from a historical copying process just like the one that produced the Eames chair. But this difference between the genuine Eames chair and its look-alike would be a difference that made no difference, that entrained no further properties in either chair; the laws of nature simply are not sensitive to bare numerical identities. So "kinds" is an exaggeration. But there is an important truth here. It is that in studying highly specific copied kinds, we should *act as if* part of what constitutes membership in that kind is a descent from numerically just *that* historical copying process. For in this way we will focus our study on individual copied items that may bear to one another qualitative similarities we did not originally know to look for. Copied items that stem from numerically the same copying process may resemble each other in *many* details of historically proper placement, or of copied qualitative "shape," some of which we did not initially recognize.

My mention of Millikan's "historical kinds" has a second motivation as well. Part of Millikan's motivation for endorsing historical kinds comes from a conviction that biological species must, in some way, be genuine kinds in nature. I have announced my sympathy with this conviction; at the start of this chapter, I indicated I would try to defend the idea that human beings compose a natural kind unto themselves, and so likewise for other biological species. But Millikan is right to suppose that some unexpected philosophical argument is needed to defend such a claim. The protracted criticism of "essentialism" in biology has shown that there are no qualitative phenotypic traits that we can warrantedly expect to crop up in all and only the members of Homo sapiens, or of any other biological species (Dupré 1981; Rosenberg 1985, pp. 180–225; Hull 1992; Sober 1992). Nor does it help, at least not in any straightforward way, to look to the genomes of members of our lineage. There are not even any genotypic features—at least, no features specifiable in qualitative biochemical terms—that crop up in all and only the members of Homo sapiens. Can we defend the idea that human beings compose a natural kind by noting that they compose one of Millikan's *historical* kinds? No, since *coming-from-numerically-just-that-origin* could not be tied, by laws of nature, to any other properties incorporated in an essential nature. Could we argue that human beings compose a *copied* kind? No, for reasons I have elsewhere identified (Elder 1996, pp. 200–201). But there is an unexpected philosophical move that does succeed, I believe. The "working" genotypic parts of all genomes in our lineage—the parts that are not just "junk DNA"—all do have something distinctive in common. This "something" is not qualitative but dispositional. These parts can to a striking degree be randomly combined with the working parts that are found at other loci, within the gene pool of our historical lineage, to produce viable organisms. Now the mention here of "our historical lineage" may seem to turn Homo sapiens into a historical kind after all, but really does not do so, since its function is just reference fixing. Compare the picture that some readers take from Kripke (1972) and Putnam (1975): namely, that we fix the reference of "water" by saying "water is just *that* physical stuff which shares the microstructure of the stuff that happens to be present in *those* samples in *those* locations." This may render it a necessary truth that water is H_2O; it does not render it a necessary truth that water is found just where those samples are.

7.5   Useless Artifacts and Useful Copyings

My main concern in 7.3 and 7.4 was with a question of specificity. Is every kind of artifact for which there is a sortal in common usage a copied kind in its own right, or is a sortal more likely to pick out a true copied kind, the less its extension is sprawling and diverse? My overall contention was that in general, the more crisply defined classes of artifacts are more likely to be copied kinds. But let me now balance that suggestion with a cautionary note about certain specifically delimited classes of copied items.

We copy from one another, half knowingly and half unwittingly, a thousand minor details of personal behavior—turns of phrase, bodily gestures, styles of dress and articles of personal ornamentation. Much of this copying is entirely uninfluenced by any history of function that the items copied may have. The psychological and social mechanisms that underlie the copying are either sensitive to past functionality only sometimes—perhaps mainly in larger and more consequential aspects of behavior—or are distinct from the mechanisms that underlie function-sensitive copying of cultural items. Or, indeed, the copying may occur because there is a function served by the copying itself—for example, that it affirms group affiliation—rather than by the items copied. In any case familiar artifacts such as neckties, high-heeled shoes, and nose rings are very unlikely to amount to copied kinds. The behaviors of wearing such personal articles may fall into copied kinds, but the articles themselves probably do not.

The main reason for this is that members of true copied kinds have a characteristic shape—in a literal or metaphorical sense—and replication of that shape causally depends on something that previous members of the kind did in consequence of having that shape. Now neckties (for example) do literally have a typical shape: a necktie typically is shaped like two elongated kites joined at the tail. But what causes that shape to get replicated, in one bolt of silk after another, is not some performance that earlier neckties were disposed by their shape to carry out. The causes that produce new neckties have nothing to do with performances that past neckties, as physical objects, effected. That is why neckties can vary widely in width, can have parallel sides, can get fashioned from a wide variety of materials, and why inferences from the shape of this year's neckties to the shape of neckties in 2010 will only accidentally be accurate. In contrast, the ways in which neckties get knotted around the neck, and the circumstances in which neckties thus knotted get displayed, actually *are* matters over which we may run inferences that non-accidentally succeed. The reason why is that it is *wearings of* neckties that form a true copied kind. These have a characteristic physical and social "shape," and get reproduced because, in the historically proper placement of a specific dress code, they have afforded their agents social access or acceptance. Ontologically, there are manufactured materials such as silk and cotton yarn, themselves both secondary substances and copied kinds; these materials exist in spatially localized quantities, and of these there are some shaped like two elongated kites joined at the tail; and there are wearings of neckties. That is all. The expanses of silk or of cotton yarn (etc.) that satisfy the sortal "neckties" do not have essential properties distinct from those of any other parcels of these materials. Like any such expanses, they essentially are characterized only by the properties essentially characteristic of silk and of cotton themselves. These expanses do not amount to unitary matter-objects that trace out spatiotemporal careers of their own.

7.6   The Problem with Projectivism: Customs and Conventions

If there really are in the world instances of copied kinds, there are in the world at least some artifacts. So any philosopher who holds that artifacts do not, in ontological strictness, exist, must deny that copied kinds are instanced in the world. At the same time such a philosopher must allow that we *project* onto the world existences of artifacts—creations of artifacts, courses of existence which they trace out, destructions of artifacts. What elements in the world act on us to cause this projection, according to such a philosopher? The only plausible answers must cite our customs or conventions or linguistic practices. But the arena of custom and convention and language is rife with copied kinds, as I now briefly shall argue. If this is correct, the ontology of *projectivism with respect to artifacts* is incoherent.

Consider, to begin with, some typical customs. It is customary among many peoples to mark national holidays with public spectacles or the singing of patriotic songs. There are customary ways of preparing meals, there is a custom of taking a siesta, and there is a custom of bringing casseroles to the homes of people recently bereaved. It seems hard to doubt that at least part of what causes such patterns of behavior to get copied from person to person, and from generation to generation, is some function that the patterns have repeatedly, if not invariably, served. Thus such copied patterns have not only a characteristic "shape" but also, it seems, a proper function. It is no objection to this claim that different patterns or practices could have served the same function as well. So long as we are confident that the mechanisms that copied these behaviors would have copied them (perhaps actually *did* copy them) more widely than behaviors that served no function, or served the same functions less well, or served functions less useful, the attribution of proper function is warranted. Moreover, these customary behaviors serve functions only when and as cued to customarily recognized settings—to holidays, to meal times, to members of the family of the deceased—and can therefore be said to have historically proper placements. At least many customs, it seems, are copied kinds.

To call a copied pattern of behavior a "convention," in contrast, often is to suggest that it *lacks* a proper function. It is a convention in countries other than England, Australia, and Japan to drive on the right side of the road. But obviously right-side driving is not intrinsically useful, nor is driving on the left intrinsically a poorer practice. It is a convention to say "hello" when answering the phone, to extend one's right hand when greeting someone, and to call a chair "a chair"—but in all of these cases the intrinsic content of the act confers by itself no benefit or gain. But coincident with every case of such conventionally copied behavior there is something that does have a proper function and is a member of a copied kind. It is that same behavior relationally described—that behavior *as* a copying, *as* a replicating of conventional behavior. *Replicating* right-side driving, where right-side driving already has the status of a widespread behavior, copied from person to person over long periods, is indeed extremely useful. Replicating an *expected* sound by saying "hello"—as opposed to producing just that sound for its own sake—is indeed useful. *Followings of* conventions have specific shapes, they often have proper functions, and they have historically established conventional settings. They too are then copied kinds.

Finally, a word about linguistic practices. There has been considerable debate as to whether, and in what sense, language is governed by conventions (see Millikan forthcoming b). Whatever the outcome of this debate, it seems virtually certain that at least sometimes some linguistic patterns get copied in consequence of functions that earlier tokens of those patterns have served, and that the copying is cued to contexts similar to those of the earlier tokens. If so, there are in our linguistic behavior tokens of copied kinds: the current copyings have a characteristic "shape," a proper function, and a historically proper placement.

Why Austerity in Ontology Does Not Work: The Importance of Biological Causation

In part II, I defended familiar objects against what I regard as the main reasons for doubting their reality, namely the worries about causal exclusion and about compositional vagueness. In chapter 7, I argued that these defenses, if successful, apply to many familiar artifacts and biological devices as well as to the familiar objects more often cited in discussions of natural kinds and real essences. But what should a philosopher think who has nagging doubts whether my defenses *are* successful, whether they can be extended to accommodate rebuttals I have not foreseen, and so forth? Is it the wiser philosophical strategy to undertake other defenses of the ontological credentials of familiar objects—or to retreat to a restricted ontology in which familiar objects take no place? In this chapter I argue in favor of the former response.

But certainly it is the latter response that would reflect the prevailing trend in contemporary metaphysics. Austerity in ontology might almost be said to be, in Kuhn's sense, the dominant paradigm. On one contemporary view there are in the world no objects at all (Hawthorne and Cortens 1995); on another, only a single scattered object (Horgan and Potrč 2000); on another, only a single primal stuff, scattered in various parcels (Sidelle 1989, pp. 54–55; Jubien 1993); on another, only filled regions of space-time (Heller 1990). More generous ontologies picture the world as composed of only microparticles (Unger 1979b, p. 234; Wheeler 1979, p. 166; Rosen and Dorr forthcoming), or only of microparticles together with all mereological sums of microparticles,[1] or only of physical simples that future science may substitute for the microparticles currently recognized.

The problem with all such austere ontologies, I will argue in this chapter, is that they cannot adequately explain how it can *appear* that the world contains far more objects than, according to these ontologies, really exist. How can it appear that there are in the world compositionally vague objects, if sorites arguments entail that compositionally vague objects cannot really exist? How can it appear that there are objects composed wholly of microparticles, if the fact that microphysics is closed and complete—or close enough—entails that those objects cannot really act? Almost all proponents of austere ontologies do recognize the force of these questions. Almost all maintain, in response, that the sentences expressing those appearances are true, even though what makes them true are states of affairs involving far simpler objects. Thus it is said that the sentence "there are chairs in this room" can well be true, but that what makes it true—what it reports—is that certain physical simples are arranged chair-wise (van Inwagen 1990, pp. 101 ff.; cf. Hawthorne and Michael 1996). Now earlier chapters in this book have provided reasons for doubting whether austere ontologists *can* consistently offer paraphrases for such sentences, such that they are true of the world in all its (alleged) austerity. Concerning this particular paraphrase of "there are chairs in this room," for example, chapter 3 argued that an ontologist who holds that there are strictly no chairs must also hold that there is strictly no such phenomenon as simples' being chair-wise arranged. But the reason I have provided for questioning the paraphrases doubles as my reason for denying that causal exclusion arguments impugn the ontological credentials of familiar objects (chapter 4). And in this chapter I am addressing philosophers who have misgivings about my response to such arguments. So in this chapter I will allow, for the sake of argument, that some of the austere ontologist's paraphrases may be successful. The austere ontologist *can* explain, I will allow, how it can appear to be the case that "there are chairs" and "there are human beings" are true: these sentences *are* true, I will let the austere ontologist claim, and misleading only if taken at face value as revealing truths about ontology.

But what if we set aside the sentences which express particular appearances which the world presents to scientifically informed common sense, and look instead at the fact itself that the world does *appear*, in any way at all, to scientifically informed common sense? I call this a "fact" since it seems that even the most austere ontologist could not plausibly deny that the world does objectively appear, at least to many minds, as richer than the austere ontology reports it to be. But if the world objectively appears as richer than it really is, there must objectively exist in the world minds to which it so appears. Perhaps these minds do not fully answer to the understanding of minds that is incorporated in scientifically informed common sense itself; the austere ontologist can reserve the option of denying, for example, that "folk psychology" is a true theory of what our minds are like. He may even elect to follow the lead of eliminative materialists and deny that scientifically informed common sense is a body of *beliefs* (Churchland 1981). But he must, I contend, find some way of recognizing those states in us that his austere ontology corrects or supplants. He must at least say, in effect, "there objectively are minds in the world, occupying states that I must at present rather misleadingly characterize as mistaken beliefs, and the function of my ontology is to replace some of these states with other states that for now I must characterize as more accurate beliefs."

Yet *minds* of any sort—whether folk-psychological minds or minds answering to Churchland-style materialism—are not visibly included on the list typically offered by austere ontologists of what, in ontological strictness, exists in the world. Then *can* austere ontologists consistently allow that the world appears to be as rich as common sense supposes?

To be sure, if the austere ontologist can paraphrase "there are three chairs in this room" so that it comes out as objectively true, of the world as it is in all its austerity, so too might he claim to paraphrase "there are minds in the world" so that it comes out objectively true of the world as it really is. But what *else* might the austere ontologist be required to say about minds, other than just that they exist? Minds have thoughts, and thoughts have contents, and the austere ontologist must have latitude enough to embrace a plausible theory of thought content—of what it is for a given thought to be a thought *that* such-and-such, a thought *about* so-and-so. (I am assuming that we have not so sharpened specialization in philosophy as to turn it into intellectual irresponsibility.) Yet the only plausible theory of thought content, I shall argue, compatible with two forms of fallibility which obviously characterize us—fallibility in our standing judgements about what nature's kinds are like, and fallibility in our occasion indexed judgements that this or that kind is now present before us—is a theory that views minds as the products of a selectional history. It follows that the austere ontologist cannot *merely* allow that "minds exist" is objectively true of the world. He must further allow, as objectively true, that minds are characterized by devices and programs that are "supposed to" operate in certain ways—that they are found in medium-sized objects fashioned by natural selection. Indeed to assert the objective existence of minds as sophisticated as ours—minds capable of holding the beliefs about microparticles and about natural selection itself that are incorporated in scientifically informed common sense—the austere ontologist must also, as I shall argue, concede that these minds are members of linguistic communities.

Now in one way this challenge may seem trifling. If the austere ontologist can devise paraphrases of "chairs exist" and "minds exist" so that these come out as objectively true of the austere world he believes in, so too, it may seem, can he devise paraphrases for "DNA exists," "organisms exist," and "linguistic communities exist." The real problem, however, is that the ontologist must do more than allow that such existence claims are true. He must also find room—if the arguments I will offer are correct—to recognize causal transactions *between* genes and organisms and populations. For any story of natural selection, as chapter 5 reminds us, talks about ways random mutations in genes *cause* members of a species to have certain new traits, and about ways the presence in those members of those traits *causes* the spread, through the gene pool of that species, of those advantageous genes. This is causation at the macro level: causation exercised by, and affecting, familiar medium-sized objects. It is exactly the sort of causation that the austere ontologist must reckon to be *excluded* by causation at the level of microparticles—provided, that is, he elects not to join me in defending medium-sized objects against causal exclusion arguments. My contention is that minds, specifically our minds, are literally and strictly the products of natural selection. The austere ontologist must deny that *there are* products of natural selection—that natural selection *produces* anything—so long as he retains the conviction that motivates his austerity, namely, that all real causation is causation at the level of microparticles.

8.1   Can Austere Ontologists Put Minds on the Ground Floor of Reality?

The austere ontologist must, I have said, allow that there are minds in the world, specifically *our* minds, to which it appears that the world contains the rich range of objects which scientifically informed common sense believes in. What he must deny is, as I shall argue, the best theory we have of what it is for those minds to have states with content—of what it is for those minds to *be* minds. The minds the austere ontologist believes in must be unshaped by selectional history. They must indeed be very close to the "transcendental subjects" affirmed by Kant and Husserl. My claim is that this shows that austere ontologists must endorse an unscientific, indeed an antiscientific, understanding of the nature of our minds. To some friends of austerity this may actually seem an inconclusive indictment. But I shall take it as condemnation enough.

It may be useful for me to frame my indictment of austere ontology in broad historical terms. It is an idea as old as ontology itself that important elements of the world, which to common sense seem perfectly real in their own right, are but projections or shadows cast by more fundamental, self-standing elements. Plato arguably held that the whole world of particulars in space and time is a shadow cast by the Forms, ultimately by the One, onto a version of the Indefinite Dyad (Findlay 1974). Hegel maintained that nature is the self-projection of the Absolute Idea into a phase of self-externality, which the life of Spirit shows to be more apparent than real (Hegel 1970, §244; 1975, §376). But there is a problem with assigning *minds* to the bedrock position in such a projective scheme (as students of Kant and Husserl know well).[2] Minds are by nature entangled with too many other elements and structures in the world. You cannot just pluck minds from the manifest image, and place them on the ground floor of reality, if your intention is to declare significant other elements of the manifest image (e.g., familiar medium-sized objects) to be mere projections of the minds: the other elements will cling to the minds during the move, or else the minds you end up with will be eviscerated, "minds" in name only. That, at least, is what I shall argue.

In the next section I will present arguments to the effect that minds are by nature the products of a selectional history, and that *our* minds are by nature the products of a history of *natural* selection. In the section following I shall argue that minds as sophisticated as ours must be members of a plurality of minds united by a common language. Hence as much of the physical world will cling to our minds, during their move to a projective position, as is needed to keep them distinct from one another—think of the "subtle bodies" that Aquinas required to keep the angels distinct from one another—and as is needed to enable them to communicate with one another; moreover, as much of the social world will cling to the minds as is needed to cement the relations needed for languages to emerge and to exist.

8.2   A Theory of Content That Allows for Fallibility

The premise from which I argue that minds are by nature the products of a selectional history is that minds—certainly our minds, but also any others that are "minds" in an interesting sense—are in two ways fallible in their judgments about the surrounding world. On the one hand we minds are vulnerable to holding mistaken beliefs as to what the kinds and stuffs that surround us are stably and standingly like, what they are like by nature. Indeed we commonly *discover* this: our experience commonly teaches us that our previous beliefs of this sort were inaccurate or incomplete, as when we learn that plants of a certain kind are nutritious only when mature, toxic when newly sprouted, or when we learn that water will actually expand in volume when it freezes. On the other hand we are vulnerable to mistakes in reidentifying nature's kinds and stuffs, as when we judge that the plant in front of us belongs to a familiar edible kind when really is of a toxic kind, or when we suppose that the shiny pebbles in the creek are gold when really they are iron pyrites.

Recent views on the content of thought have generally made one of these two forms of fallibility understandable by rendering the other form puzzling. Suppose for example that what makes this or that concept be a concept *of* this or that stuff or kind is a match that obtains between a description we entertain—a description we associate with the concept, or a description that just *is* the concept—and the stuff or kind in question (see Millikan 2000, sec. 3.5). Then fallibility in a judgment such as "this is skunk cabbage" or "this is a lizard" is easy to understand: in making such a judgment we are asserting a particular description of an object in front of us which in fact does not satisfy the description. But what then happens to fallibility in the beliefs we hold as to what a given kind or stuff is like by nature—fallibility, in other words, in the description itself which shapes the reference of our concept? Since being-referred-to by the concept just *is* answering to whatever description we entertain for kind or stuff in question, the description is bound to be accurate of whatever kind or stuff (if any) the concept refers to—and since in all counterfactual scenarios a slice of the world need *only* answer to the description we entertain, in order to fall in the extension of that concept, that description will be moreover complete, it will capture all the features that that kind or stuff is bound to have.

So a description theory for thought content will have most of the counterintuitive consequences which Kripke attributes to the parallel description theory for public-language names (Kripke 1972). Each of us will have a curious arm-chair infallibility about the essential properties of any kind or stuff he or she thinks about. The implausibility of this view can be diminished by holding that reference, for a concept, requires a match with only "a weighted 'most'" of the properties featured in the description—diminished, but not removed. The description theory still cannot squarely admit that each of us can learn from experience that this or that kind or stuff has by nature many properties we earlier did not suspect it to have, or that the kind or stuff can on occasion lack many properties we earlier supposed it to have by nature.

The main rival to a description theory of thought content, at least until recently, has been a causal theory (see, e.g., Putnam 1975). What it is for a concept of mine to pick out a particular kind or stuff in nature, on this alternative approach, is for identifications employing that concept to be caused, triggered in me, by the presence before me of just that kind or stuff. Such a view promises to make it crystal clear how any of us might be mistaken, even massively mistaken, about what the kinds and sorts which we identify are like by nature. For how any of us gets *caused* to employ a given concept, in a judgment about what now is before us, is not in general a matter we can determine by armchair reflection—yet it does determine, on this view, what slice of the world that concept is a concept of. But this clarity on how we could be wrong in the standing beliefs we hold about nature's kinds and stuffs is bought at the cost of utter darkness about our fallibility in judgments as to when those kinds and stuffs are present before us. Any such judgment, after all, is caused. If diverse causes can get us to employ a given concept in judgments about what is before us—if (token) judgments that, in mentalese orthography, all look like "this is a cow" can get caused often by cows, but sometimes by horses or even by dogs—then what follows is that that concept is a concept of a disjunctive kind. But *all* identifications employing that concept will be *correct*, indeed inevitably correct.

This problem, called "the disjunction problem," appears to be as fatal to causal theories of thought content as Kripkean objections are to a description theory of thought content. Jerry Fodor, who has perhaps best set forth "the disjunction problem," has indeed offered a solution (Fodor 1992, ch. 3 and ch. 4, in particular pp. 91 ff.). Fodor's solution hinges on "assymetrical dependence": mentalese tokens of "cow" refer to cows, not indiscriminately to cows-or-horses-or-dogs, just in case *if* there had been no cow-caused tokens of "cow," there *would have been* no horse- or dog-caused tokens, but not vice versa. But there is a principled obstacle to this solution. If such assymetrical dependence holds, it is equally true that *if* there had been no *cow-or*-horse-or-dog caused tokens of "cow," there *would have been* no horse- or dog-caused tokens—from which it would follow that "cow" refers after all to cows-or-horses-or-dogs. The jury is still out on whether this obstacle can be surmounted (cf. Fodor 1992, p. 121 ff.); this chapter will assume that the prospects are poor.

But recent work in philosophy of mind has shown that if we look to the selectional history of the devices and programs in us that fashion our identifications of nature's kinds and stuffs, we can find a way around the disjunction problem, while retaining an externalism about thought content rather like that of the causal theory (Millikan 1989; Elder 1998b). Begin by considering the classic victim of the disjunction problem, *Rana pipiens*. The visual system of this species of frog repeatedly tokens neural signals that trigger motor routines which launch the frog, mouth open and tongue extended, on a gulping lunge in one direction or other, depending on features of the neural signal. What does the neural signal represent? The system that produces it is not particularly discriminating: it can be triggered by flies crossing the space close to the frog's eyes, but also by bits of leaf and even by BBs. The causal theory suggests that the signal's content is the disjunctive kind "fleebees," that is, flies or BBs or bits of leaf or. . . .

But what was the system that produces this signal selected for doing, on the reasonable assumption that there is something for which it was selected? This question can yield an answer to "the disjunction problem," I hold, but only if answered carefully. The answer is *not*, I contend, that the system was selected for signaling the presence in the frog's immediate environment of flies, or of flies or BBs, or of anything else—or at least not *merely* for that. That a device *merely* signals how matters stand with the outside environment confers on its owners no reproductive advantage, and bestows on the genes that code for it no greater fitness than their alleles have. Devices that signal how matters stand in the nearby environment do confer an advantage but only to the extent that they get *used* or *responded to* by other devices, often within the same organism, whose performance will be improved if adjusted to those outside matters. Just so here. The system that produces the famous neural signals in *Rana pipiens* was selected for because of the ways actual (token) signals, which it historically produced, switched on and steered gulping routines within the host frogs.

Thus the proper function of this system is enabling *other* biological devices, namely, these motor routines, to perform *their* proper function. That passing flies historically caused this system to issue the famous neural signals tells us not so much *what* that system's proper function is, as *how* it has served its proper function. And so in general for selected devices that signal in response to features of the environment. Their proper function is switching on and steering "consumer devices," often in the same organism. But devices that can do this job flexibly enough for evolution to like them, and simply enough for evolution to be able to devise them, are ones that do it in a special *way*—by issuing signals that correspond, at least often enough, to *values of* the relevant outside features.

Now, can these reflections lay the disjunction problem to rest? It all depends, some philosophers would hold, on what the proper function is of the motor routines themselves that launch the frog's gulps. Historically these routines caused host frogs to ingest a huge group of small dark moving objects, many but not all of which were flies or other nutritious (to frogs) insects. Then is the proper function of these motor routines to effect ingestion of *small dark moving objects*? In that case, the system that produces the famous neural impulse must have enabled these routines to serve *their* proper functions by matching its outputs to *small dark moving objects*—be they flies or BBs or bits of leaf. The content of the neural impulse remains disjunctive.

The crucial question here, I have argued (Elder 1998b), is what causally explains the proliferation among *Rana pipiens'* ancestors of just these gulping routines—what causally explains the fact that genes coding for these routines won out over their alleles. Even if we are ignorant of some details, we can be sure that in this causal explanation, the *darkness* of the bits ingested plays no part. Neither does their *movingness* (-prior-to-ingestion). What figures in the causal explanation, we can be sure, is just the *nutritiousness* (to frogs) of the bits ingested. So the proper function of the motor routines is effecting ingestion of nutritious bits. And the famous neural signal enabled the routines to do this just to the extent that it corresponded to the presence of nutritious bits. Therefore the content of that signal is "nutritious bit here now."

The disjunction problem *can* then really be solved, in the case of its most famous victim. Viewing the devices that produce and respond to the famous neural signal *as products of natural selection* permits us to see that what that signal is *supposed to* correspond to—its content—is not just everything in the environment that *does* in fact trigger its production. It permits us to understand how the frog can make wrong identifications of the small bits that cross its visual field.

Can these insights be extended? Can we devise an externalist picture of the content of *our* thoughts, thus preserving clarity on how we can be fallible about the nature of the kinds and stuffs we encounter, while invoking selectional history to explain our fallibility in the judgements we make as to when particular kinds and stuffs are present before us? The answer is Yes, provided we are careful to admit just how far the extension must reach. Ruth Millikan *has* extended the teleosemantic account to cover the content of our thoughts (Millikan 1984, 2000). The extension does have to reach far— too far for me to trace it in a chapter (or even in *several* chapters). The reason *why* the extension must reach far is that *Rana pipiens's* famous neural signal is designed to steer only a single behavior, to steer it always, and to steer it immediately. It is as much a command—"gulp thataway!"—as an indicative report—"nutritious bit over there!" *Our* thoughts about our surroundings can be exclusively *indicative* reports. They can be stored for later use, and when used can be enlisted to attune actions that serve any of a range of desires. But the ways our indicative thoughts guide and shape our behaviors, as effectively as evolution has required them to do—or better, as effectively as evolution has required of the cognitive and sensory programs that produce them—has much in common with the ways the neural signaler in *Rana pipiens* won the favor of natural selection. Our indicative thoughts have shaped behaviors effectively, as often as they have been required to, by corresponding under definite mapping rules to a variety of ambient circumstances. They have not always shaped behaviors effectively, and do not do so now: the outside circumstances which the rules require the thoughts to map may be absent; we are fallible, both in our thoughts about what nature's kinds are like, and in our thoughts about when they are present before us. But natural selection has never insisted on perfection.

8.3   Collective Cognitive Tracking

I now have sketched the reasons for thinking that if minds are placed on the ground floor in a projective ontological scheme—if we allow, as austere ontologists must, that the world really appears to minds to contain many familiar medium-sized objects, but say that the medium-sized objects are all *mere* appearances, projected by the minds onto a world that is far more austere—then those minds must drag with them enough of biological reality to populate a whole history of natural selection. They must likewise, and for the same reason, drag with them the causation by which they are naturally selected. I now will argue that if the world is objectively to appear as rich as *scientifically informed* common sense supposes it to be, the minds on the ground floor must be minds *in a community*. They must drag with them enough physical reality to secure their mutual distinctness and enable them to communicate linguistically with one another, and enough social reality to undergird the existence of a shared language.

Our hominid ancestors, though individually weak, were able to fell prey that was stronger, faster, and better protected with claws and scales. The standard explanation is that our hominid ancestors hunted in groups. It may come closer to the standpoint of the prey to say that our ancestors, when hunting, formed a single scattered individual—one composed of six or ten hominid-shaped parts, all responding in stunning coordination not just to the prey's movement but even to its posture and its behavior. What effected the distinctive coordination among our hominid ancestors was language.

Early history also presented our ancestors with a need to do cognitive tracking—to reidentify the various kinds and stuffs of nature not just across different spatial locations but across different states of affairs. They needed to learn that the fruits that now tasted so delicious were the very ones that recently were green and small, or that the plants that produced those pink flowers were the very ones that, when chewed, relieved aches and pains. It would have been good strategy for nature to equip our ancestors with endowments for *collective* cognitive tracking parallel to those for collective hunting—with endowments for communicating their several reidentifications of a given kind to one another linguistically, by appending different predicates to a common term for that kind (see Millikan 2000, chaps. 5 and 6).

After all, many of the kinds and stuffs of nature present a variety of shifting appearances, and unmistakably display distinctive markings only in rare circumstances or under tests that cannot routinely be conducted. There is a need to gather together diverse marks by which such kinds and stuffs can be identified in different contexts, even if none of the marks is by itself a perfectly reliable indicator, and this need is best met by having separate trackers communicate to one another in language the marks that, as they separately discover, cling to members of the kind. Some trackers may concentrate on scents or calls, others on visual appearances, others on distinctive behaviors, others literally on tracks. Some may concentrate on the same kind of marks as the others, but from different perspectives and locations. In the end these trackers may associate a common description with the term they use to designate the kind, and may share a common battery of tests for tracing its presence. But in the beginning of collective cognitive tracking, different trackers will associate different overall descriptions with the term in question, and will cue at least some of their tokenings of the term to different sorts of observations. This is indeed the best strategy for nature to elect, if collective cognitive tracking is to succeed when performed by trackers who initially have only limited repertoires of ways of spotting any one of nature's kinds and stuffs. For language can ensure that success by any *one* tracker, at spotting the kind in a particular context, will amount to success by *all* at spotting the kind there. So nature's aim of maximizing aggregate reidentifications of the kind among members of the group— and with it, successes in each member of the programs within himself that rely on reidentification of that kind—is best served if there is a *diversity* of contexts in which individual members are disposed to recognize that kind, and a *diversity* of tests on which the members rely.

To put it differently, linguistic representations of how the world is, just like indicative thoughts about how the world is, have it as their proper function to attune their recipients' behaviors so as to facilitate satisfaction of their recipients' desires. But indicative reports that I receive from my fellow speakers can do this job even better, in my own case, than indicative thoughts that I token in my own head. A main *way* they do this job better is by being cued to *a wider range* of ways of tracking the kind or stuff that is their subject matter, than I myself wield for tracking that kind or stuff. And that happens just because my fellow speakers cue their identifications of the kind or stuff in question to different marks and features from those used by me and by other individual speakers.

Thus for tokens of a term for a given kind to be coreferential, it is not in general necessary that the tokeners associate a common description with the term. We can abandon the strikingly artificial suggestion, essential to the description theory of reference for public language designators, that *all* competent users of, say, "gold" associate the same description with gold (see Kripke 1972), or that there is a single description, aptly referred to as "the watery role," which all users of "water" believe water to fulfill.[3] We divide the labor of devising tests for tracking nature's kinds and stuffs. We *must* divide the labor in the case of kinds and stuffs that present diverse appearances in different settings, often resemble other kinds, and present distinctive marks only to extended observation or unusual vantage points. As thinkers who eventually learn reliable and fairly complete descriptions of such hard-to-track kinds, we *must* be members of linguistic communities.

Our participation in collective cognitive tracking also explains another feature of the use of public language designators, which seemed so puzzling and odd when Kripke first posed it as a problem for the description theory of their reference. This is that a speaker who copies his tokens of a designator from tokens uttered by his fellow speakers can somehow borrow reference for those tokens even though he himself associates almost no individuating descriptions with the designator, and possibly no *true* individuating descriptions at all. I can in this way borrow the reference of "Einstein," even though I associate only the false belief that Einstein was the inventor of the atomic bomb (Kripke 1972); I will not indeed be in a position to say much *about* Einstein, apart from asking just who he was and when he lived, but at least the questions I ask will truly be questions *about Einstein*, the real Einstein. And just so I can borrow reference for the name of a phenomenon, for example, "nuclear fission," or for a kind, for example, "sulfuric acid," despite myself entertaining few true, and no true individuating, descriptions of what they designate.

The explanation of how this can happen is that we are equipped with programs for collective cognitive tracking that allow for maximum participation. *Any* speaker who copies from fellow speakers his tokens of a term designating a kind or a stuff or an individual in nature, and presents understandable sentences[4] featuring the tokens to fellow speakers, can qualify as a participant in collective cognitive tracking. For that is the best strategy for nature to elect. From nature's point of view, collective cognitive tracking works better when a greater number of trackers can contribute to and benefit from it. For the greater that number, the greater the number of agents whose behavior can be attuned, in the greater number of ways, to how matters stand with the kind (or stuff or individual) that is tracked.

Individually, our endowments permit us to track only poorly, across states of affairs, the more subtle kinds and stuffs and phenomena of nature—those that are of particular interest to scientifically informed common sense. Yet we do track them well, and attune our actions and practices to their ways and natures; we manage to form precisely the body of belief that *is* scientifically informed common sense. We can do this only because we are members of linguistic communities.

8.4   Conclusion

The type of ontology that this chapter seeks to discourage could be sloganized as: "In the beginning was The Austere, and The Austere appeared otherwise than it really was." My objection has been that this claim cannot be right, since it is badly incomplete. In the beginning—on the ground level of ontology—there must also be that to which The Austere appears as it does. But this additional element is not a transcendental subject, nor several, but a linguistic community of naturally selected minds. So it is false that in the beginning there was (only) The Austere. In the beginning—on the ground floor of ontology—there is the splendidly, marvelously rich.

Notes

Chapter 1

1. This is a slight oversimplification. Strictly, chromium is also found in Turkey and in the Phillipines.

2. As to Sidelle, this is only his *initial* formulation of what we know about chemical kinds. "I have proceeded by giving the conventionalist's story in the material mode," he then remarks; ". . . The conventions, of course, are in the first instance rules governing the use of terms, or kinds of terms, and I may have gotten myself into some trouble by proceeding at the object level" (1989, p. 43). Sidelle's preferred formulation, for reasons I make clear below, is that the extra premise is something we know about the proper use of *terms for* chemical kinds.

3. Sidelle 1989, p. 55n., p. 57; 1998, pp. 441–444; cf. Jubien 1993. "World-stuff" is from Hawthorne and Cortens 1995.

4. Michael Rea puts forth much the same paradox in Rea 2002, ch. 7. But Rea's paradox concerns temporal priority, not logical priority, and it is presented as a paradox confronting *naturalists*—for Rea argues that the only tenable position a naturalist can take on modality is conventionalism.

Chapter 2

1. Hegel 1975, secs. 89–98, or Hegel 1969, pp. 109–137 and pp. 600–622; Aristotle 1966, *Physics*, Bk. I, ch. 5, or Bk. V, ch. 1 and ch. 5. Recent philosophers who have *not* overlooked the importance of contrariety include

Millikan 1984, pp. 268–271, and chaps. 16 and 18; Bradley 1893, Bk. 1, ch. 3; Johnson 1921, part I, ch. 11.

2. This reasoning would seem to be the motivation behind Stephen Schwartz's contention that genuine natural kinds—as opposed to mere nominal kinds—must be the subjects of "stable generalizations" (Schwartz 1980). For Mill's claim about natural kinds, see Mill 1973, p. 122.

3. When, for example, sodium-20 undergoes beta-delayed alpha emission, what remains is oxygen-16, which has higher positive valence. When beta plus decay happens to carbon-11, what remains is boron-11, and boron has a higher negative valence (*Encyclopaedia Britannica*, fifteenth ed. [1974], pp. 436 and 438).

Chapter 3

1. This version is *modeled after* Peter van Inwagen's position on what really happens, in ontological strictness, when it appears that a familiar object (e.g., a chair) is destroyed (van Inwagen 1990, pp. 98–99 and 158). But it is not *the same as* van Inwagen's position, since van Inwagen draws a distinction between familiar objects which are not organisms, and familiar objects which (like Max) are organisms. Organisms, for van Inwagen, really do exist, and so the apparent destruction of Max would be a destruction in all ontological strictness. But van Inwagen's conviction that organisms exist derives from a curious argument which moves from Cartesian premises about *his own* existence to the un-Cartesian conclusion that he exists *as an organism* (1990, Section 12). It is therefore unsurprising that some philosophers influenced by van Inwagen, e.g., Rosen and Dorr (forthcoming), take the view the apparent destruction of *any* familiar object, including any organism, is just a rearrangement of simples.

2. Thus, Armstrong: If objects a and b both exist, Armstrong says, it would be arbitrary to deny that the fusion of a and b also exists, since saying that it exists really adds nothing to the claims that a exists and that b does—it is, in Armstrong's phrase, an "ontological free lunch" (Armstrong 1997, pp. 12–13 and 185). Lewis's argument for fusions is more complex: no principled reason can be given why an arbitrarily assembled aggregate of microparticles does not compose an object, while the aggregate composing some familiar object does exist, since only a vague boundary can be drawn between the microparticles within some familiar object and those without it, and real objects cannot be vaguely delimited (Lewis 1986b, pp. 212–213). But even this argument starts with a shift in the burden of proof. The ques-

tion Lewis addresses is how composition (into objects) can be "restricted" to just familiar objects.

3. See B225, A183 / B226–A186 / B229, A187 / B230, and B233. But in other passages Kant appears to allow that individual substances—the word "substance" now appears in the plural—can pass out of existence, and that what is necessary is just that some substances persist and overlap in their careers. See Strawson 1966, pp. 128–131.

4. *Metaphysics* Zeta 3, 1029a1–27; cf. Theta 7, 1049a22–36. On Aristotle's ambivalence concerning prime matter, see Owens 1978, pp. 330–335.

Chapter 4

1. For example, Bontly 2002; Sturgeon 1998, e.g., at p. 418 ("a physicalism that is both general and severe"); and Yablo 1992.

2. Jaegwon Kim's widely known presentation of the causal exclusion worry goes just a bit differently. To have caused James's arrival at Supermarket S, Kim would say, James's decision about the best price on pork chops would have had to cause the complex sequence of microparticle movements that subvened his arrival at Supermarket S (Kim 1998, pp. 35 ff.). But the set of microparticle movements that *subvened his decision* has, itself, an unassailable claim to having caused the arrival-subvening sequence. So, barring causal overdetermination, the decision cannot itself have caused that sequence, and hence cannot really have caused the arrival at Supermarket S. Where my presentation differs is in avoiding the sort of claim presented in the first sentence. Stephen Yablo has shown that causes must be "commensurate" with their effects (Yablo 1992), and from this it follows that the first sentence may voice an *unfair, exaggerated* requirement. *Of course* James's decision was not sufficient to ensure just *that* microparticle version of the arrival at the supermarket; at best, it sufficed to ensure the occurrence of *some* microparticle version *or other* of an arrival-at-Supermarket-S.

3. I think there is some reason to prefer the view that the relata are states of affairs over the view that they are Kim-style events; see Elder 2001a, p. 115. But the reason is a fairly minor one, and it is less cumbersome to speak of the relata as being Kim-style events; so that is how I shall speak of them.

4. This sort of claim is suggested by Jaegwon Kim as a legitimate response to causal exclusion arguments. For though Kim sets forth such arguments as clearly and forcefully as anyone, the conclusion he draws from them is

not simply that mental events are causally inefficacious. Rather his conclusion is that *either* the effects that mental events appear to produce really are produced by microparticles instead, *or* there is no question of "instead"—the occurrence of a particular mental event just *is* the instantiation of some highly disjunctive microphysical property. See Kim 1989a and 1989b, or Kim 1999.

5. Owens takes *coincidence* to be conceptually prior to *cause*: on his analysis, a cause is that which "ensures that its effects are no coincidence" (1992, p. 2). There is one merely apparent problem with this analysis, and one real one. The merely apparent problem is that such-and-such outcomes qualify as *c's effects* only if c qualifies as their cause, and the analysis therefore smuggles the analysandum into the analysans. This problem is merely apparent since "its effects" can be read just referentially, not attributively: it serves to point out *those* outcomes, outcomes that in fact will turn out to be *c's* effects. The real problem is that "ensures" means "brings it about that," on all plausible readings, and so *c's* being a cause is being analyzed by *c's* causing something. Probably the charitable reading is that by "ensures" Owens means something closer to "is." That is, a cause is that in virtue of which its effects are no coincidence. That the effects all occur *would* be a coincidence, the thinking would run, if there were not some common circumstance necessary and sufficient for all of them—or, more liberally, some common necessary condition for them or some common sufficient condition (p. 24)—and so *c* is what keeps by effects from being coincidental by *being* that common Necessary and Sufficient (or Necessary, or Sufficient) condition. This reading takes Owens's analysis to be close to the analysis I endorse. (But not close enough: Owens still would not be in a position to offer the argument against transitivity that I give in the next paragraph, or the argument against agglomerativity that I offer in 4.4.) But it would be strikingly inconsistent with Owens's tolerance of agglomerated necessary and sufficient conditions, and his consequent concession (ibid., p. 22) that there are necessary and sufficient conditions for coincidences.

Chapter 5

1. David Armstrong espouses a modest physicalism (see, for example, 1997, p. 153), though some of his formulations may sound like hegemonic physicalism instead (e.g. p. 6 or p. 253).

2. Jaegwon Kim sets forth the best-known arguments for hegemonic physicalism, but his own position, as I said in ch. 4 fn. 4, is somewhat hedged:

either the causings reported by the special sciences really are done by collections of microparticles instead, or there is no question of "instead"—the causes identified by the special sciences *are* just a matter of such collections of microparticles coming to satisfy very complex microphysical descriptions. See Kim 1989a, 1989b, or 1999.

Chapter 6

1. Here is the worst of these objections—the only one to which I cannot envision any answer at all. The "degrees of truth" theorist will probably want, the objection begins, to say that what is objectively fixed, for sentences about familiar objects, are only the *relations* "_____ is true to a greater degree than . . ." and "_____ is true to a lesser degree than. . . ." In other words, only *ordinal* degrees of truth are objectively fixed. As to *cardinal* degrees of truth—e.g., " 'B is a bicycle' is true to degree 0.862, where 1.0 is the value for perfect truth"—the degrees theorist will probably want to say they inevitably involve a measure of arbitrariness. Different cardinal values can legitimately be assigned, the degrees theorist will want to say, so long as the relations are all preserved; any such assignment is as objectively correct as any other. But now comes the objection (from Keefe 1999). There are intuitively legitimate ways of reassigning cardinal values to atomic statements that result in flip-flops in ordinal values in pairs of nonatomic statements, or pairs joining a nonatomic statement to an atomic one. For example, there is a legitimate reassignment of cardinal values for p and q that moves p from being less true than $p \rightarrow q$ to being more true than $p \rightarrow q$. The only reply we degrees theorists can make, so far as I can see, is to say that there simply is no objective fact of the matter as to the relations of *being true to a greater degree than* that obtain between pairs of nonatomic statements or pairs joining a nonatomic statement to an atomic one. But this reply involves a subtle abandonment of truth-functionality for nonatomic statements. Truth-functionality *is* preserved for the *cardinal* degrees of truth for all statements, atomic and nonatomic. But those aren't the degrees of truth that really matter, that are objectively fixed, according to us degree theorists. It is the *ordinal* degrees of truth that are objectively fixed, we say. But now we are forced to say that these are fixed for atomic statements and not for nonatomic ones, e.g., those involving the connective "$\rightarrow$." This abandons truth functionality.

Chapter 7

1. Any historical account of proper function, like the one I take over from Millikan, faces a "poser" concerning the very first item from which a copied kind comes to be copied. An example: didn't the very first telephone, fashioned by Alexander Graham Bell, already have a proper function (Plantinga 1993, p. 203)? From Millikan's perspective (to which I subscribe) the answer is "Yes and No." The first telephone had no direct proper function, but it did have an adapted and derived proper function—that of enabling remote conversation. In just the same way, if a chameleon turns a shade of puce unprecedented in chameleon history, its skin color has an adapted and derived proper function—that of matching its puce surroundings (Millikan 1984, ch. 2). "Derived" here means that the telephone or the skin color inherits its proper function from that of the program in Bell, or the device in the chameleon, which produced it. In Bell's case, the derivation probably extends further still: beyond the program that underlay production of the telephone, to a program for forming such programs, and perhaps to a capacity for forming programs for forming programs. The derivation ends at a device that operates independently of Bell's conscious intentions, and which has a direct proper function. This brings up the "poser" concerning the proper function of the first item from which a *biological* copied kind comes to be copied. Suppose the first wings (tokens) arose as a result of a single, massive mutation. Didn't those very first wings already have a proper function? But there is no intuitive pressure on Millikan to answer Yes. The onset of (direct) proper function, she can plausibly reply, depends on the intensity of selectional pressure on the gene pool. It depends on how soon the capacity for flight, bestowed by early wings, conferred replicative advantage on the genes which coded for wings—and replicative disadvantage on the alleles. This is a causal question. The answer to it—and to the question where (direct) proper function begins—may be somewhat vague. But it would be poor practice to throw out causation, or the theory of natural selection, out of preference for a neatly segmented universe.

2. I say "historically proper *placement*" rather than "environment" because the latter suggests a *broad* cross-section of the historical surroundings; placement is a matter of co-location, and consequent cooperation, with tokens of *specific* other copied kinds.

3. Much the same point is made by Ned Block (1997) in his discussion of "the Disney Principle."

Chapter 8

1. I infer that this view has proponents from the fact that it is the intersection of two widely held views: the belief that all there is in the world, in ontological strictness, are the microparticles posited by physics; and the belief in mereological universalism (also known as unrestricted mereological composition). Alan Sidelle reviews the considerations that lead philosophers to the former belief in section Sidelle 1998, § V, and adds that "these philosophers are not small in number" (p. 440). A representative defense of mereological universalism is Rea 1998.

2. One good place to see a representative problem cropping up for Husserl is Husserl 1970, sec. 61. One good place to see a similar representative problem for Kant is in the first *Critique*, at the bottom of A 534 / B 562, when compared with the second sentence on A 541 / B 569, and with A 545 / B 573 (*"Nun tut ihm . . ."*), and with the very start of A 550 / B 578 (in the Kemp Smith translation, p. 465 as compared with pp. 469, 471, and 474).

3. See Jackson 1998. Jackson contends that his position, viz. that terms such as "water" have "A-extension" in addition to the more familiar "C-extension," is distinct from the description theory of reference. But his contention seems to me unsupported.

4. The speaker does have to know the right *sorts* of questions to ask, in order for the tokens of a term in his sentences to corefer with tokens of that term as uttered by fellow speakers. In Millikan's parlance, he must wield a "template" of the item referred to, an outline of the *sorts* of properties with respect to which it is stably and determinately characterized (Millikan 2000, ch. 5). But note that the idea of a "template" is *not* the idea of a description (via determinables) that all intelligent users of a term associate with the term, and which affords a priori knowledge about the referent. For some or all elements of a template are revisable in the face of experience (ibid., p. 30), and differences in personal experience may lead one speaker to associate a detailed template, another a more sketchy template, while yet both utter tokens of a common term that are perfectly coreferential (ch. 5).

References

Adams, Robert. 1995. "Introductory Note to *1970," in Feferman, Solomon, et al., eds., *Kurt Gödel: Collected Works, Vol. III*. Oxford: Oxford University Press.

Aristotle. 1966. *The Basic Works of Aristotle*. Ed. Richard Mckeon. New York: Random House.

Armstrong, David. 1978. *Universals and Scientific Realism, vol. II: A Theory of Universals*. Cambridge: Cambridge University Press.

———. 1988. "Are Quantities Relations? A Reply to Bigelow and Pargetter." *Philosophical Studies* 54, pp. 311–315.

———. 1997. *A World of States of Affairs*. Cambridge: Cambridge University Press.

Bennett, Jonathan. 1988. *Events and their Names*. Indianapolis: Hackett.

Bigelow, John, and Pargetter, Robert. 1990. *Science and Necessity*. Cambridge: Cambridge University Press.

Block, Ned. 1997. "Anti-Reductionism Slaps Back," in Tomberlin 1997.

Bontly, Thomas. 2002. "The Supervenience Argument Generalizes." *Philosophical Studies* 109, pp. 75–96.

Bradley, F. H. 1893. *Appearance and Reality*. Oxford: Clarendon Press.

Churchland, Paul. 1981. "Eliminative Materialism and the Propositional Attitudes." *Journal of Philosophy* 78, pp. 67–90.

Clark, Austen. 2000. *A Theory of Sentience*. Oxford: Oxford University Press.

Davidson, Donald. 1967. "Causal Relations." *Journal of Philosophy* 64, pp. 691–703.

———. 1969. "The Individuation of Events," in Rescher 1969.

———. 1970. "Mental Events," in Foster, Lawrence, and Swanson, J. W., *Experience and Theory*. Amherst: University of Massachusetts Press.

Dawkins, Richard. 1982. *The Extended Phenotype*. Oxford: W. H. Freeman.

Dummett, Michael. 1973. *Frege*. New York: Harper and Row.

Dupré, John. 1981. "Natural Kinds and Biological Taxa." *Philosophical Review* 90, pp. 66–90.

Elder, Crawford. 1994. "Laws, Natures, and Contingent Necessities." *Philosophy and Phenomenological Research* 54, pp. 649–667.

———. 1995. "A Different Kind of Natural Kind." *Australasian Journal of Philosophy* 73, pp. 516–531.

———. 1996. "On the Reality of Medium-Sized Objects." *Philosophical Studies* 83, pp. 191–211.

———. 1998a. "Essential Properties and Coinciding Objects." *Philosophy and Phenomenological Research* 58, pp. 317–331.

———. 1998b. "What versus How in Naturally Selected Representations." *Mind* 107, pp. 349–363.

———. 2001a. "Mental Causation versus Physical Causation: No Contest." *Philosophy and Phenomenological Research* 62, pp. 111–127.

———. 2001b. "Materialism and the Mediated Causation of Behavior." *Philosophical Studies* 103, pp. 165–175.

Ereshefsky, Marc, ed., 1992. *The Units of Evolution*. Cambridge, Mass.: MIT Press.

Findlay, J. N. 1974. *Plato: the Written and Unwritten Doctrines*. New York: Humanities Press.

Fodor, Jerry. 1992. *A Theory of Content and Other Essays*. Cambridge, Mass.: MIT Press.

———. 1997. "Special Sciences: Still Autonomous After All These Years," in Tomberlin 1997.

Hawthorne, John O'Leary, and Cortens, Andrew. 1995. "Towards Ontological Nihilism." *Philosophical Studies* 79, pp. 143–165.

————. and Michael, Michaelis. 1996. "Compatibilist Semantics in Metaphysics: A Case Study." *Australasian Journal of Philosophy* 74, pp. 117–134.

Hegel, G. W. F. 1969. *Science of Logic*. Trans. A. V. Miller. London: George Allen and Unwin.

————. 1970. *Philosophy of Nature*. Trans. A. V. Miller. Oxford: Oxford University Press.

————. 1975. *Encyclopaedia of the Philosophical Sciences*, Part I: Logic. Trans. William Wallace. Oxford: Oxford University Press.

Heil, John, and Mele, Alfred. 1993. *Mental Causation*. Oxford: Oxford University Press.

Heller, Mark. 1990. *The Ontology of Physical Objects: Four Dimensional Hunks of Matter*. Cambridge: Cambridge University Press.

Horgan, Terry and Potrč, Matjaž 2000. "Blobjectivism and Indirect Correspondence." *Facta Philosophica* 2, pp. 249–270.

Hull, David. 1992. "The Effect of Essentialism on Taxonomy: Two Thousand Years of Stasis," in Ereshefsky.

Husserl, Edmund. 1970. *Cartesian Meditations*, trans. Dorion Cairns. The Hague: Martinus Nijhoff.

Jackson, Frank. 1998. *From Metaphysics to Ethics*. Oxford: Oxford University Press.

Johnson, W. E. 1921. *Logic*. Cambridge: Cambridge University Press.

Johnston, Mark. 1997. "Manifest Kinds." *Journal of Philosophy* 94, pp. 564–583.

Jubien, Michael. 1993. *Ontology, Modality, and the Fallacy of Reference*. Cambridge University Press.

Kant, Immanuel. 1929. *Critique of Pure Reason*. Trans. Norman Kemp Smith. London: Macmillan.

Keefe, Roseanna. 1999. "Vagueness by Numbers." *Mind* 107, pp. 565–579.

Kim, Jaegwon. 1969. "Events and their Descriptions," in Rescher 1969.

————. 1980. "Events as Property Exemplifications," in Brand, Miles, and Walton, D., *Action Theory*. Dordrecht: D. Reidel.

————. 1989a. "The Myth of Nonreductive Materialism." *Proceedings and Addresses of the American Philosophical Association* 63, pp. 31–47.

————. 1989b. "Mechanism, Purpose, and Explanatory Exclusion." *Philosophical Perspectives* 3, pp. 77–108.

————. 1998. *Supervenience and Mind*. Cambridge, Mass.: MIT Press.

————. 1999. "Making Sense of Emergence." *Philosophical Studies* 95, pp. 3–36.

Kripke, Saul. 1972. *Naming and Necessity*. Cambridge, Mass:. Harvard University Press.

Lewis, David. 1973. *Counterfactuals*. Cambridge, Mass.: Harvard University Press.

————. 1986a. *Philosophical Papers,* vol. II. Oxford: Oxford University Press.

————. 1986b. *On the Plurality of Worlds*. Oxford: Blackwell.

Loewer, Barry. 1996. "Humean Supervenience." *Philosophical Topics* 24, pp. 101–128.

Macdonald, Cynthia, and Macdonald, Graham. 1995. *Philosophy of Psychology*. Oxford: Blackwell.

Mackie, J. L. 1965. "Causes and Conditions." *American Philosophical Quarterly* 2.4, pp. 245–264.

McGinn, Colin. 1981. "Modal Reality," in Richard Healey, ed., *Reduction, Time, and Reality*. Cambridge: Cambridge University Press.

McLaughlin, Brian. 1993. "On Davidson's Response to the Charge of Epiphenomenalism," in Heil and Mele 1993.

Markosian, Ned. 1998. "Brutal Composition." *Philosophical Studies* 92, pp. 211–249.

Merricks, Trenton. 2001. *Objects and Persons*. Oxford: Oxford University Press.

Mill, J. S. 1973. *A System of Logic*, in J. M. Robson, ed., *Collected Works of John Stuart Mill*. Toronto: University of Toronto Press.

Millikan, Ruth. 1984. *Language, Thought, and Other Biological Categories*. Cambridge, Mass.: MIT Press.

————. 1989. "Biosemantics." *Journal of Philosophy* 86, pp. 281–297.

————. 1999. "Historical Kinds and the Special Sciences." *Philosophical Studies* 95, pp. 45–65.

————. 2000. *On Clear and Confused Ideas*. Cambridge: Cambridge University Press.

————. forthcoming a. "Biofunctions: Two Paradigms," in Cummins, Ariew, and Perlman, eds., *Functions in Philosophy of Biology and Philosophy of Psychology*. Oxford: Oxford University Press.

————. forthcoming b. "In Defense of Public Language". Antony and Hornstein, eds., *Chomsky and His Critics*. Oxford: Blackwell.

Moore, G. E. 1925. "A Defence of Common Sense," in J. H. Muirhead, ed., *Contemporary British Philosophy*. London: Allen & Unwin.

Neander, Karen. 1995. "Misrepresenting and Malfunctioning". *Philosophical Studies* 79, pp. 109–141.

Owens, David. 1992. *Causes and Coincidences*. Cambridge: Cambridge University Press.

Owens, Joseph. 1978. *The Doctrine of Being in the Aristotelian Metaphysics*. Toronto: Pontifical Institute of Mediaeval Studies.

Plantinga, Alvin. 1993. *Warrant and Proper Function*. Oxford: Oxford University Press.

Putnam, Hilary. 1975. "The Meaning of 'Meaning'," in *Minnesota Studies in the Philosophy of Science VII: Language, Mind, and Knowledge*, ed., Keith Gunderson. Minneapolis: University of Minnesota Press.

————. 1977. "Realism and Reason." *Proceedings and Addresses of the American Philosophical Association* 50.

————. 1981. *Reason, Truth, and History*. Cambridge: Cambridge University Press.

————. 1982. "Why There Isn't a Ready-Made World." *Synthese* 51, pp. 141–167.

Rea, Michael. 1997. *Material Constitution: a Reader*. Lanham, Maryland: Rowman and Littlefield.

————. 1998. "In Defense of Mereological Universalism." *Philosophy and Phenomenological Research* 58, pp. 347–360.

————. 2002. *World Without Design*. Oxford: Oxford University Press.

Rescher, Nicholas et al. 1969. *Essays in Honor of Carl Hempel*. Dordrecht: D. Reidel.

Rosen, Gideon and Dorr, Cian. forthcoming. "Composition as a Fiction." www.nyu.edu/gsas/dept/philo/faculty/dorr.

Rosenberg, Alexander. 1985. *The Structure of Biological Science*. Cambridge: Cambridge University Press.

Schwartz, Stephen. 1980. "Natural Kinds and Nominal Kinds." *Mind* 89, pp. 182–195.

Sellars, Wilfrid. 1963. "Philosophy and the Scientific Image of Man," in his *Science, Perception and Reality*. London: Routledge and Kegan Paul.

Sidelle, Alan. 1989. *Necessity, Essence, and Individuation*. Ithaca: Cornell University Press.

———. 1998. "A Sweater Unraveled: Following One Thread of Thought for Avoiding Coincident Entities." *Nous* 32, pp. 423–448.

Sider, Theodore. 1997. "Four-Dimensionalism." *Philosophical Review* 106, pp. 197–231.

Sober, Elliott. 1992. "Evolution, Population Thinking, and Essentialism," in Ereshefsky 1992.

Sorabji, Richard. 1980. *Necessity, Cause and Blame*. Ithaca: Cornell University Press.

Sorensen, Roy. 1988. *Blind Spots*. Oxford: Oxford University Press.

———. 1998. "Sharp Boundaries for Blobs." *Philosophical Studies* 91, pp. 275–295.

Strawson, Peter. 1966. *The Bounds of Sense*. London: Methuen.

Sturgeon, Scott. 1998. "Physicalism and Overdetermination." *Mind* 107, pp. 411–432.

Tomberlin, James, ed., 1997. *Philosophical Perspectives 11: Mind, Causation, and World*. Oxford: Blackwell.

Unger, Peter. 1979a. "There Are No Ordinary Things." *Synthese* 41, pp. 117–154.

———. 1979b. "I Do Not Exist," in G. P. Macdonald, ed., *Perception and Identity*. Ithaca: Cornell University Press.

———. 1979c. "Why There Are No People," in Peter A. French, Theodore E. Uehling, Jr., and Howard K. Wettstein, eds., *Midwest Studies in Philosophy IV: Studies in Metaphysics*. Minneapolis: University of Minnesota Press.

————. 1980. "The Problem of the Many," in Peter A. French, Theodore E. Uehling, Jr., and Howard K. Wettstein, eds., *Midwest Studies in Philosophy, V: Studies in Epistemology.* Minneapolis: University of Minnesota Press.

van Inwagen, Peter. 1990. *Material Beings.* Cornell University Press.

Wheeler, Samuel. 1979. "On That Which Is Not." *Synthese* 41, pp. 155–173.

Williamson, Timothy. 1994. *Vagueness.* London and New York: Routledge.

Wittgenstein, Ludwig. 1929. "Some Remarks on Logical Form." *Proceedings of the Aristotelian Society*, Supp. Vol. 9, pp. 162–171.

Wittmer, D. Gene. 1998. "What Is Wrong with the Manifestability Argument from Supervenience." *Australasian Journal of Philosophy* 76, pp. 84–89.

Woodward, James. 1992. "Realism about Laws." *Erkenntnis* 36, pp. 181–218.

Yablo, Stephen. 1992. "Mental Causation." *Philosophical Review* 101, pp. 245–280.

Zimmerman, Dean. 1995. "Theories of Masses and Problems of Constitution." *Philosophical Review* 104, pp. 53–110.

Index